AF269931

THE LINKEDIN PLAYBOOK FOR EMPLOYEES

THE LINKEDIN PLAYBOOK FOR EMPLOYEES

How to Build Your Professional Brand Without Losing Your Job

JAMES CHEO

LinkedIn Top Voice

WILEY

Registered Offices
John Wiley & Sons, Inc., 111 River Street, Hoboken, NJ 07030, USA
John Wiley & Sons Ltd, New Era House, 8 Oldlands Way, Bognor Regis, West Sussex, PO22 9NQ, UK

For details of our global editorial offices, customer services, and more information about Wiley products visit us at www.wiley.com.

The manufacturer's authorized representative according to the EU General Product Safety Regulation is Wiley-VCH GmbH, Boschstr. 12, 69469 Weinheim, Germany, e-mail: Product_Safety@wiley.com.

Wiley also publishes its books in a variety of electronic formats and by print-on-demand. Some content that appears in standard print versions of this book may not be available in other formats.

Library of Congress Cataloging-in-Publication Data is Available:

ISBN 9781394362400 (Cloth)
ISBN 9781394362424 (ePub)
ISBN 9781394362417 (ePDF)

Cover Design: Wiley
Cover Image: © EyeEm Mobile GmbH/Getty Images
Author Photo: Courtesy of James Cheo

Set in 10/15pt Adobe Garamond Pro by Straive, Chennai, India.
SKY10152011_040926

TABLE OF CONTENTS AND WHAT YOU'LL DISCOVER

How to Use This Book

IF YOU'RE STARTING FROM ZERO: Read straight through. Parts build sequentially—foundation → profile → content → technical → community → conversion → sustainability.

IF YOU'RE POSTING BUT NOT GETTING RESULTS: Start with Part III (Content Strategy) and Part IV (Technical Excellence). Refine what and how you post.

IF YOU'RE GETTING VISIBILITY BUT NO OPPORTUNITIES: Jump to Part VI (Conversion). Learn to measure what matters and translate attention into outcomes.

IF YOU'RE BURNING OUT: Go to Part VII (Sustainability), then circle back to Part I to reconnect with purpose.

IF YOU NEED QUICK WINS: Use the Appendix—seven practical resources you can implement today.

Three Promises This Book Makes

✘ This book will NOT teach you to game algorithms. Algorithms change. Human psychology doesn't. You'll write for the brain.

✘ This book will NOT turn you into an influencer. You're an employee. Your goal is influence, not fame. There's a difference.

✘ This book will NOT make you go viral. Viral moments fade. Credibility compounds. You'll build something that lasts.

WHAT YOU'LL GAIN

By the end of this book, you'll have:

✓ **A profile that positions you clearly** and converts visitors into connections (Part II)

✓ **A content strategy built on three to five pillars** that give your voice structure (Part III)

✓ **Storytelling and psychology skills** to make expertise memorable (Part III)

✓ **Technical knowledge** to amplify reach efficiently (Part IV)

✓ **Community-building approach** that turns connections into relationships (Part V)

✓ **Conversion framework** that transforms visibility into career outcomes (Part VI)

✓ **Mindset and boundaries** to sustain presence for years (Part VII)

The Email That Nobody Read

There's a specific moment I remember. It was a Tuesday afternoon in 2018, and I was staring at my inbox, waiting for replies that would never come.

I'd spent three hours crafting an email about a market insight I thought was important. Something I'd noticed about sustainability trends that could reshape how we thought about our business. I'd been careful with the language, precise with the data, thoughtful about the implications. I hit send to about forty colleagues across different regions.

Silence.

Not even the courtesy of an acknowledgment. The email simply vanished into the void of corporate communication, buried under meeting invitations and budget updates and the endless digital noise that fills every professional's day.

This wasn't unusual. This was normal.

I was one employee among hundreds of thousands, scattered across time zones and continents. And I kept running into the same problem: how do you share an idea with people you'll never meet? How do you start a conversation when you can't even get into the same room?

Email wouldn't work. I couldn't CC the world.

But I wanted to contribute. Not for recognition. Not for promotion. Just to be useful. To share what I was learning in a way that might help someone else make sense of the complexity we were all navigating.

So I tried something different. I tried LinkedIn.

The Accidental Experiment

The strategy, if you could even call it that, was embarrassingly simple. Share takeaways from panels I attended. Post perspectives on market trends I was tracking. Treat the platform as an extension of what I was already doing—speaking at events, analyzing markets, trying to make sense of things.

Nothing fancy. Nothing viral. Just consistent.

My first post received eleven likes. Eight were from people I knew personally. Three were probably accidental.

But I kept going. Not because I had a grand plan, but because at least those eleven people had seen it. Which was eleven more than had read my email.

Then something shifted.

A colleague in London commented on a post about emerging markets. Someone in New York saved a framework I'd shared. A sustainability analyst I'd never met sent a message: "This helped me understand the market better. Can we talk?"

That's when I realized something that should have been obvious: LinkedIn isn't just a broadcasting tool. It's a bridge.

The Compound Effect

What happened next surprised me.

I started sharing more than market analysis. I wrote about sustainability—not just as a business trend, but as a personal conviction. I wrote about my upbringing, about the values that shaped how I think and lead today. I stopped trying to sound like a corporate spokesperson and started writing like myself.

The response was immediate. Not in scale, but in quality. People didn't just like the posts. They engaged. They disagreed. They shared their own stories. The comment sections became conversations. The conversations became relationships.

And the numbers started to compound.

From zero followers to five hundred. Then a thousand. Then five thousand. The growth wasn't linear. It was exponential. Not because I'd cracked some algorithmic code, but because I'd done something simpler: I'd been useful, repeatedly, over time.

From zero to over 80,000 followers. Over ten million views annually. LinkedIn Top Voice. Favikon ranked me top 5 in Singapore, top 26 globally for financial markets.

But here's what actually matters, and why I'm telling you this story: I'm not selling anything. I'm not an entrepreneur. I'm not building a personal brand to launch a coaching business or a consulting firm.

I'm an employee. Just like you, probably.

I just wanted a voice.

What I Learned in the Comment Sections

LinkedIn gave me something I didn't expect: an education.

The comment sections became classrooms. Every post was a focus group. I learned what people cared about—not what I assumed they cared about, but what they actually spent time thinking about. What confused them. What frustrated them. What inspired them to act.

I learned that the posts I thought were brilliant often landed flat. And the posts I almost didn't publish—the ones that felt too personal or too simple—were the ones that resonated most.

I got better. Not just at writing or communicating, but at listening. At understanding what people needed before they could articulate it. At seeing patterns across industries and roles and geographies.

And something else happened, something I didn't anticipate: I became more influential inside my own organization. Senior leaders who'd never responded to my emails were now commenting on my posts. Colleagues in different divisions were reaching out for collaboration. I wasn't more important, but I was more visible. And visibility, I learned, creates opportunity.

The Lesson

Looking back, none of this was planned. There was no strategy document. No content calendar in those early months. No growth targets or engagement metrics.

It started with one simple goal: connect better. Share useful insights. Build relationships beyond the limitations of org charts and office walls.

But it taught me something every professional should know, something that contradicts almost everything we're told about building influence in the digital age:

You don't need to be famous to be influential. You don't need to go viral to be valuable. You don't need a million followers to make an impact.

You just need to show up. Share with sincerity. Let the work accumulate.

Small actions, repeated consistently, create remarkable results.

That's the power of LinkedIn.

And that's not motivational speak. It's mathematics. It's the compound interest of professional relationships, playing out over months and years. Every thoughtful post is a deposit. Every genuine interaction builds trust. And trust, unlike algorithmic visibility, doesn't decay.

Why This Book

I'm writing this book because I keep getting asked the same question: "How did you do it?"

And the honest answer is: I didn't do anything magical. I just did something consistently.

But there were principles behind the practice. Patterns I noticed. Mistakes I made. Lessons I learned the hard way that you don't have to learn the same way.

This book is the guide I wish I'd had when I posted that first awkward update and waited nervously for someone, anyone, to respond.

It's for the employee who wants to share ideas beyond their immediate team. For the professional who knows they have something valuable to contribute but doesn't know how to get it heard. For anyone who's ever felt invisible in a large organization and wondered if there was a way to build influence without sacrificing authenticity.

It's not about gaming algorithms or chasing viral moments. It's about building something more enduring: a professional presence that reflects who you actually are, creates genuine value for others, and compounds over time into opportunities you can't yet imagine.

Because here's what that silent Tuesday afternoon in 2018 taught me: the problem wasn't that I had nothing to say. The problem was that I was using the wrong medium to say it.

LinkedIn gave me the right medium. This book will show you how to use it without losing yourself in the process.

Let's begin.

I Foundation—Why This Matters Now

That Tuesday afternoon taught me something every professional should know: the problem wasn't that I had nothing to say. The problem was that I was using the wrong medium. This section explores why LinkedIn has become that medium, how it fundamentally changed who gets to be heard, and why waiting for "perfect" is a trap. You'll discover the hidden patterns that make LinkedIn different from every other platform, understand why invisibility is costly even for talented professionals, and learn why starting before you're ready is the only way to start at all.

1 Why LinkedIn Is the Professional Network That Changed Everything

The Parking Lot Problem

On a Tuesday morning in December 2002, Reid Hoffman sat in his car in a parking lot in Mountain View, California, staring at his laptop screen. He had just sent an email to a carefully curated list of friends and former colleagues—people he'd worked with at PayPal, Apple, and SocialNet. The email contained a link to something he'd been building in secret for months: a website that would let professionals connect with each other online.

Then he waited.

His inbox remained silent. Not just for minutes, but for hours. When responses finally started appearing the next day, they were polite but puzzled. "Interesting idea," one former colleague wrote back. "But honestly, Reid, who's going to use this?"

It was a reasonable question. In 2002, the internet was still finding its identity. Social networking existed—Friendster had launched earlier that year—but the idea of bringing your professional life online seemed, to most people, somewhere between unnecessary and slightly unsettling. Your résumé was something sacred, something you printed on cream-colored paper and carried to interviews in a leather portfolio. Posting it online for anyone to see felt uncomfortably exposed, like showing up to a business meeting in your pajamas.

But Hoffman had noticed something that others hadn't. He'd spent the better part of a decade in Silicon Valley, watching how careers actually progressed, and he'd identified a pattern that contradicted everything we're taught about professional success.

The most successful people, he observed, weren't necessarily the most talented. They weren't always the hardest working. They weren't even always the smartest.

They were the most connected.

This wasn't a new insight. In 1973, a sociologist named Mark Granovetter published a paper that would become one of the most cited in social science history. He called it "The Strength of Weak Ties." Granovetter had interviewed hundreds of professional workers who'd recently changed jobs, asking a simple question: How did you hear about the position?

What he discovered was counterintuitive. People didn't get jobs through their closest friends or immediate family—the people they saw every day, their "strong ties." They got jobs through acquaintances—former colleagues, college classmates they hadn't spoken to in years, or friends of friends. Their "weak ties."

The reason was simple but profound. Your close friends know mostly the same people you know. They travel in the same circles. They have access to the same information. But your acquaintances? They bridge to entirely different networks. They know people you don't know. They hear about opportunities you'd never encounter on your own.

The problem was access. If weak ties were so valuable, how could you maintain them? How could you keep track of hundreds of acquaintances scattered across companies, cities, and countries? How could you signal to them what you were working on, what opportunities you were seeking, and what value you could provide?

Sitting in that parking lot, reading those polite but skeptical responses, Hoffman was trying to solve what we might call the "weak tie problem." Could you build a platform that made maintaining weak ties not just possible, but effortless? Could you give everyone access to the network effects that had previously been reserved for those lucky enough to attend the right schools or work at the right companies?

That parking lot moment was the beginning of LinkedIn. But what happened next would take twenty years to unfold, and it would fundamentally change not just how professionals network, but how we think about expertise, authority, and career advancement in the digital age.

The Résumé Trap

When LinkedIn launched publicly in May 2003, it attracted exactly the audience you'd expect: recruiters searching for candidates, job seekers building their profiles, and networking-obsessed executives collecting connections like baseball cards. Within twelve months, the platform reached one million users.

But here's what's interesting: despite that growth, LinkedIn wasn't actually solving the problem Hoffman had identified.

It had become a digital Rolodex—a place to store business cards. A résumé repository that you updated once a year if you were diligent, or once every five years if you were like most people.

The infrastructure for weak ties was there—you could connect with former colleagues, add your college classmates, and find people you'd met at conferences. But then what? The platform was fundamentally static. You could see where people worked, what their job titles were, and which schools they'd attended. But you couldn't see what they were thinking about, working on, struggling with, and learning from.

In his groundbreaking book *Bowling Alone*, political scientist Robert Putnam documented the decline of what he called "social capital" in American life. Between 1970 and 2000, participation in civic organizations, community groups, and even informal social gatherings had plummeted. Putnam's theory was that as we became more mobile, more suburban, and more digital, we were losing the casual connections that historically provided the foundation for both personal well-being and professional opportunity.

LinkedIn had theoretically solved this problem by moving professional networking online. But in practice, it had simply digitized the résumé without addressing the deeper issue: How do you build real relationships through a screen? How do you demonstrate expertise to people who've never met you? How do you turn a connection into a conversation?

For nearly a decade, these questions went unanswered. LinkedIn grew—10 million users by 2007, and 100 million by 2011—but it grew as infrastructure, not as innovation. When the company went public on the New York Stock Exchange in May 2011, it was validating a business model, not a revolution.

The platform had created the pipes. But there was no water flowing through them.

The Influencer Accident

In 2012, LinkedIn's product team launched what looked like a marketing stunt.

They invited a small group of high-profile business leaders—Richard Branson, Arianna Huffington, and Bill Gates, people whose names alone guaranteed attention—to start publishing long-form articles directly on the platform. They called it the Influencers Program.

The logic seemed straightforward enough: If you could read Richard Branson's thoughts on entrepreneurship without leaving LinkedIn, you might spend more time on the platform. More time meant more engagement. More engagement meant more advertising revenue. It was platform economics 101.

But what actually happened was far more interesting.

Within weeks, something unexpected began to emerge. The articles these influencers published weren't just being read—they were sparking conversations. Comment threads stretched into the hundreds. People weren't passively consuming content; they were debating it, building on it, and using it as a launching point for their own ideas.

More importantly, ordinary users started asking a question that LinkedIn's product team hadn't anticipated: "If Richard Branson can share his insights here, why can't I?"

This is what we might call an "inflection point"—a moment when a system tips from one state to another. In this case, LinkedIn was tipping from a network platform to a content platform. And nobody, least of all LinkedIn itself, quite understood what that meant.

By 2015, LinkedIn had opened publishing to everyone and added analytics that showed creators exactly which posts were resonating and why. For the first time, professionals could treat LinkedIn like a laboratory—posting ideas, measuring response, and refining their message based on real-time feedback.

What emerged was something unprecedented in professional life: a meritocracy of ideas.

Think about how expertise traditionally worked. If you wanted to be recognized as a thought leader in your field, you needed credentials: a PhD, a bestselling book, a position at a prestigious company, or a speaking slot at a major conference. These barriers to entry weren't just high—they were gatekept by a small group of institutions and individuals who decided whose ideas deserved amplification.

LinkedIn didn't eliminate those advantages entirely. But it created an alternative path. An analyst at a mid-sized consulting firm could publish an insight about organizational behavior that reached more people than a *Harvard Business Review* article. A product manager at a startup could share a framework that influenced how thousands of people thought about product development. A junior employee could write something thoughtful and watch it spread not because of their title, but because of the value it provided.

For the first time in professional history, distribution was democratic. You didn't need permission. You just needed something worth saying.

The Microsoft Multiplier

Then came 2016, and with it a transaction that would cement LinkedIn's transformation.

Microsoft acquired LinkedIn for $26.2 billion—at the time, one of the largest tech acquisitions in history. Tech journalists speculated about synergies. They wrote about data integration, about advertising possibilities, and about how Microsoft could leverage LinkedIn's network for its enterprise software ambitions.

But what Microsoft really bought was legitimacy.

Consider what happened next. LinkedIn wasn't just a social network anymore. It was infrastructure. It was integrated into Outlook, into Teams, into Office 365. When you drafted an email to someone you'd never met, LinkedIn would surface their profile, their interests, and their recent posts. When you joined a video call, you could see the LinkedIn profiles of other participants. When you applied for a job, employers expected—assumed—that you had a complete LinkedIn profile.

The platform had become essential. Not optional. Not experimental. Essential.

And here's where the network effects that Hoffman had imagined back in that parking lot finally, fully kicked in. As more professionals joined because LinkedIn was now part of their daily workflow, more value accrued to existing members. As more companies integrated LinkedIn into their hiring and business development processes, more professionals had to maintain active presences. As more professionals shared insights, more people came to read them, which encouraged more sharing.

In economics, this is called a "positive feedback loop." In plain English: success breeds success.

But the Microsoft acquisition did something else, something subtle but crucial. It signaled that professional networking—and professional content creation—wasn't a fad. It was a permanent feature of modern work life.

The Democratization

Between 2019 and 2021, LinkedIn made a series of moves that completed its transformation from résumé database to professional media platform.

Creator Mode gave everyone the tools that had previously been reserved for "Influencers." Newsletters allowed any user to build a subscriber base. Live video let professionals broadcast their expertise in real time. Analytics became more sophisticated, showing not just how many people viewed your content, but who they were, where they worked, and what they cared about.

What began as Richard Branson's privilege became everyone's opportunity.

This is when LinkedIn's identity fundamentally shifted. In 2021, the platform launched the Top Voices Program—recognition not for those with the most followers, but for those who consistently added value to professional conversations. The message was explicit: LinkedIn was rewarding contribution, not celebrity.

Today, LinkedIn reports over one billion users across 200 countries. But that number doesn't capture what's actually changed.

What's changed is this: For the first time in professional history, an employee at a regional accounting firm has the same potential access to a professional audience as a Fortune 500 CEO. A product manager with no Ivy League credentials can build thought leadership that rivals tenured business school professors. A mid-level analyst can share an insight that changes how thousands of people think about their work.

The platform hasn't just grown. It has fundamentally altered who gets to be heard.

The Trust Paradox

But here's where LinkedIn's story gets really interesting, because it reveals something counterintuitive about how trust works in professional contexts.

In 2019, Edelman's Trust Barometer—an annual survey that measures how much people trust various institutions and figures—published results that should have shocked corporate communications departments everywhere.

When asked who they trusted most to tell them the truth about a company, respondents ranked regular employees significantly higher than CEOs. Not slightly higher. Significantly higher.

Think about why this matters on LinkedIn. When a CEO posts about their company's values or achievements, readers instinctively discount the message. Of course the CEO is going to present the company in the best light. They have to. But when a regular employee shares an insight from their work, readers assume they're getting something closer to truth. The employee has less to gain from spin and more credibility from proximity to actual work.

This creates what we might call the "employee advantage" on LinkedIn. As an employee, you're automatically more trusted than executives. Your insights carry more weight because they're not perceived as marketing. Your stories feel more authentic because they're not filtered through corporate communications.

On most platforms, anonymity or celebrity drives engagement. On LinkedIn, it's authenticity anchored in professional identity: your real name, your actual job, and your verifiable experience.

This is why LinkedIn isn't like other social networks. On Twitter, a viral moment can make you famous for a day. On Instagram, aesthetic appeal can build a following. On TikTok, entertainment is currency.

But on LinkedIn, what travels is usefulness. The posts that succeed aren't the funniest or most provocative—they're the most helpful: frameworks people save, insights that change how they think, and stories that help them navigate their own challenges.

The platform rewards depth over drama, expertise over entertainment, and contribution over celebrity.

The Living Résumé

Here's what this means practically:

Every comment you leave on someone else's post signals that you're engaged in professional conversations. Every article you share demonstrates your interests and judgment. Every post you publish builds evidence of how you think and what you know.

Over time, this creates what we might call a "living résumé"—a dynamic record not of what you've done, but of how you think. It shows not just your past accomplishments, but your current capabilities. Not just your credentials, but your contributions.

And here's why that matters: In a world where job tenures are shrinking, skills become obsolete faster than degrees can be earned, companies reorganize constantly, and entire industries transform overnight, the most valuable professional asset isn't your current position—it's your portable reputation.

Can people see how you think? Do they trust your judgment? Have you demonstrated expertise in public, verifiable ways? When someone googles your name, do they find evidence that you know what you're talking about?

That's what LinkedIn enables. And it's available not just to executives or entrepreneurs, but to anyone willing to share what they're learning, anyone with insights worth offering, and anyone who understands that professional success today is built not on secrecy but on generosity.

The Quiet Revolution

Reid Hoffman, sitting in that parking lot in 2002, reading those skeptical responses to his launch email, couldn't have predicted any of this.

He knew that professional networks were valuable. He knew that weak ties created opportunity. He understood that the internet could solve the "access problem" that had historically limited who could build influential networks.

But what he couldn't have foreseen was that the real value wouldn't come from the connections themselves. It would come from what people did with those connections. It would come from the conversations: from the junior analyst who shares a framework that helps thousands of people think more clearly, from the product manager who writes honestly about a failed launch and what it taught her, and from the engineer who explains a technical concept so well that non-technical colleagues finally understand it.

LinkedIn didn't just scale professional networking. It scaled professional thinking.

In Malcom Gladwell's book *The Tipping Point*, he described how social epidemics work—how ideas, products, and behaviors spread through populations. There are three key agents: Connectors (people who know everyone), Mavens (people who know everything), and Salesmen (people who can persuade).

LinkedIn collapsed these categories. On the platform, you can be all three at once. Your network makes you a Connector. Your expertise makes you a Maven. Your ability to communicate clearly makes you a Salesman. And because all of this happens in public, in a searchable, shareable format, the effects compound over time.

That's not just the best professional network. That's a fundamental shift in how professional capital is built, maintained, and deployed.

The Employee Moment

Which brings us back to you.

If you're an employee—not an entrepreneur, not an executive, and not a self-employed consultant or influencer—LinkedIn offers something unprecedented: the power to build professional visibility without leaving your job, establish expertise without starting a company, and create opportunity without sacrificing stability.

You don't need a personal brand built on selling courses or building a consultancy. You need professional presence built on sharing what you know, helping others navigate what you've navigated, contributing to conversations in your field.

And because LinkedIn is designed for professional context—because it's anchored in real identity and real work—you can do this without sacrificing credibility, without crossing boundaries, and without your contributions being mistaken for self-promotion.

The platform gives you what every professional needs, but few have historically possessed: a voice that reaches beyond your immediate circle, that survives job changes and industry shifts, and that compounds over time into something more valuable than any single position or title.

Professional capital. Portable reputation. Network effects at scale.

That parking lot conversation in 2002 was about solving a technical problem: how to help professionals maintain weak ties in a digital world.

But what emerged was something bigger. A platform that democratized not just networking, but expertise itself. A space where being helpful is the same as being successful, where contribution matters more than credentials, and where your ideas can travel as far as their value can take them.

Reid Hoffman was right about weak ties. He just didn't realize he was building something that would make those ties not just accessible, but productive. Not just possible, but powerful.

The revolution wasn't in the connections.

It was in what people would choose to do with them.

The question now—sitting wherever you are, reading this—is the same question Hoffman faced in that parking lot twenty-three years ago:

What will you do with the opportunity?

2 The Cost of Invisibility (Why Professional Branding Isn't Optional)

The Water Bottle Paradox

In 2004, a business school professor named Michael Norton ran an experiment that would fundamentally challenge how we think about value.

He took two groups of students and showed them identical bottles of spring water. Same size. Same shape. Same clear liquid inside. The only difference was the label. One bottle was labeled as generic store-brand water. The other carried a premium brand name—let's call it "Glacial Peak" or something equally evocative of mountain springs and pristine sources.

Norton asked each group a simple question: How much would you pay for this bottle of water?

The students looking at the generic bottle averaged around 50 cents—a reasonable price for basic hydration. The students looking at the premium bottle? They averaged $3.50. Some went as high as $5.

Same water. Seven times the perceived value.

Norton's point wasn't about deception or marketing manipulation. It was about something more fundamental: in the absence of other information, we use brand as a proxy for quality. We have to. We can't chemically analyze every bottle of water, taste-test every option, or research the source of every spring. So we rely on shortcuts. Brand becomes signal. Story becomes substance.

What Norton discovered about water bottles applies, with uncomfortable precision, to people.

The Résumé Problem

Early in my career, I believed in a comforting fiction: that expertise speaks for itself.

I thought that if I worked hard, delivered results, and stayed focused on the work, people would naturally recognize my value. I thought competence was enough. That quality would inevitably rise to the surface, like cream in milk, through some natural sorting process that rewarded merit above all else.

This belief was wrong. Not completely wrong—competence matters, obviously—but wrong enough to be dangerous.

Here's what I learned instead: the professional world doesn't just reward expertise. It rewards visible expertise. It rewards expertise that can be clearly articulated, easily understood, and confidently communicated. It rewards expertise that comes with a story.

Without that—without what we awkwardly call "personal branding"—even exceptional professionals risk something worse than failure. They risk invisibility.

The Invisible Expert

Let me tell you about David Chen. That's not his real name, but the story is real.

David was a senior data scientist at a Fortune 500 company—PhD from Stanford, published papers, genuinely brilliant at what he did. When I met him, he'd been passed over for promotion three times in four years. Each time, the role went to someone with less technical expertise but better "executive presence"—corporate speak for "better at talking about what they do."

David was frustrated. Angry, even. "I'm better at the actual work than any of those people," he told me. "Why doesn't that matter?"

It did matter. But it didn't matter enough.

The problem wasn't David's competence. The problem was that his competence was invisible to the people making promotion decisions. He did exceptional work, but only his immediate team saw it. He had insights that could transform how the company approached data strategy, but he shared them only in small meetings with people who already knew him. He was, in the language of economics, a high-value asset with poor price discovery.

Meanwhile, his colleague Sarah—less technically skilled but better at communicating her work—was getting invited to present at leadership meetings, asked to consult on strategic initiatives, recognized as a "thought leader" in the organization. Not because she was better at data science. Because she was better at helping people understand what data science could do for them.

Sarah had a brand. David had a résumé.

The difference determined everything.

The Commodity Trap

In 1970, a marketing professor named Theodore Levitt published an article in *Harvard Business Review* with a provocative title: "Marketing Myopia." His argument was simple but profound: companies fail when they define themselves by what they make rather than by what value they provide.

A railroad company that thinks it's in the railroad business is doomed. A railroad company that thinks it's in the transportation business has a future.

The same logic applies to professionals.

If you define yourself by your job title—"data analyst," "marketing manager," or "financial advisor"—you're competing with everyone else who has that same title. You're functionally interchangeable, distinguished only by minor differences in experience, education, or seniority.

You've become a commodity.

And here's what happens when you're seen as a commodity:

First, you get chosen for efficiency, not excellence. People pick you because you're available, because you fit the budget, because you're good enough. Not because you're uniquely valuable.

Second, your voice carries less weight. Your ideas might be brilliant, but without a reputation that precedes you, they're just one opinion among many. In meetings, in strategy discussions, in moments when decisions get made, nobody thinks to ask, "What does [your name] think about this?"

Third, opportunities bypass you entirely. Decision-makers don't have time to discover hidden talent. When they need someone for a high-stakes project, a strategic initiative, or a visible role, they go with people who have already established clear value—people whose brands they recognize.

This is the hidden cost of invisibility. Not dramatic failure. Just a steady accumulation of missed opportunities, each one small enough to rationalize but large enough to matter.

The Perception Equation

Here's a truth that most professionals discover too late: Your actual value matters less than your perceived value.

Not because perception is more important than reality—it's not. But because in complex organizations, in networked economies, and in professional contexts where people are making decisions about collaborating with you, promoting you, or choosing you for opportunities, they can't directly measure your value. They have to rely on signals.

Your brand is that signal.

Think of it this way: If your actual expertise is 9/10 but your ability to communicate and position that expertise is 2/10, how will colleagues and leaders perceive your value? As 9/10 or 2/10?

The uncomfortable answer: probably 2/10.

Because they can't see the 9/10. They only experience the 2/10. And in the absence of clear signals, they fill the gap with assumptions—usually assumptions that work against you.

This isn't fair. But fairness isn't the point. Understanding how perception works is the point. Because once you understand it, you can do something about it.

The Branding Misconception

The word "branding" makes people uncomfortable, and for good reason. It conjures images of self-promotion, manufactured personalities, and LinkedIn influencers posting inspirational quotes over sunset photos.

But professional branding, done right, isn't performance. It's clarity.

It's the disciplined practice of helping people understand who you are, what you do, and why it matters. It's building a bridge between your expertise and their understanding. It's ensuring that your value isn't hidden behind jargon, obscured by humility, or lost in the noise of organizational complexity.

When someone encounters you—whether through your LinkedIn profile, a conference presentation, a project you've worked on, or even a well-crafted email—they should come away with a clear, memorable impression:

"This person knows [specific thing]. They care about [specific value]. They can help with [specific problem]."

That's it. That's the brand. Not a logo. Not a tagline. Not a polished persona. Just clarity about your unique value.

I've watched this transformation happen countless times. An analyst starts sharing insights from projects on LinkedIn—not bragging, just reflecting on what worked and what didn't. A manager begins articulating their approach to team building in a blog. A consultant starts speaking at local meetups about their area of expertise.

Nothing flashy. Nothing viral. Just consistent communication of clear value.

And over time, something shifts. Their ideas start getting cited. Their opinions start getting sought. They get invited to meetings they weren't in before, introduced to people they hadn't met, considered for opportunities they wouldn't have heard about.

Not because they suddenly became more competent—but because their competence became visible.

The Identity Insurance

In 2008, when the financial crisis hit, thousands of highly skilled professionals lost their jobs. Many spent months—sometimes years—trying to rebuild their careers.

But some rebounded remarkably quickly. Not because they were more skilled, but because they had what we might call "identity insurance."

They'd built reputations that extended beyond their job titles. They'd published insights, spoken at conferences, and maintained active professional networks. They had brands.

When they lost their positions, they didn't lose their professional identities. The person who was known as "the one who made complex data understandable" remained that person, regardless of which company employed them. The person recognized as "the expert in sustainable supply chain design" could take that expertise anywhere.

This is why professional branding isn't vanity—it's strategy. It's career insurance in a world where job security is largely extinct.

Skills become outdated. Technologies change. Markets shift. Companies restructure. But a strong professional brand—a reputation for specific expertise, a track record of clear thinking, a network that knows your value—that compounds over time rather than depreciating.

When people trust your judgment, they follow your work across jobs, industries, even entire career pivots. Your brand becomes portable capital, the most valuable asset you can build.

From Title to Purpose

Here's a test: How do people describe you when you're not in the room?

If they use your job title—"She's a project manager" or "He's in finance"—you're defined by position. You're interchangeable with everyone else who has that title.

But if they describe you by purpose—"She's the one who gets impossible projects back on track" or "He's the person who makes financial data actually useful for decision-making"—you've transcended position. You've created a brand.

Titles describe what you do. Brands describe the change you create, the value you add, and the problem you solve.

This shift from position to purpose is what separates professionals who build lasting influence from those who accumulate credentials without impact. It's what allows people to navigate career changes with confidence, because their identity isn't tied to a specific role but to a larger contribution.

For me, this evolution took years. I started as someone defined by title: "Chief Investment Officer." Over time, through consistent sharing of insights on LinkedIn—not just about markets, but about decision-making, about learning, about connecting financial thinking with larger questions of purpose and sustainability—my brand evolved into something more specific: "The person who makes investment thinking accessible and connects it to human stories."

That shift changed everything. Not what I did, but how people understood what I did. And that understanding created opportunities I couldn't have manufactured through traditional career progression.

The Generosity Principle

Here's what most people miss about professional branding: it's not about you.

It's about helping others understand how you can help them. It's an act of service, not self-promotion.

When you share insights from a project that went well, you're helping others learn from your experience. When you articulate a framework for solving a common problem, you're giving away value. When you write honestly about a failure and what you learned, you're saving others from making the same mistake.

This is why the most effective professional brands don't feel like marketing. They feel like teaching, like mentorship, and like conversation.

And paradoxically, when you stop trying to impress people and start trying to help them, your influence grows—because people can sense the difference between performance and generosity. They know when someone is promoting themselves versus when someone is contributing value.

The professionals who build the strongest brands aren't the loudest or the most polished. They're the most consistently useful.

The Google Test

Here's an exercise I recommend to every professional I work with: Google yourself.

Not out of vanity, but out of strategy. Because when someone is deciding whether to hire you, collaborate with you or promote you, that's exactly what they'll do. They'll Google you.

What will they find?

For many professionals, the answer is discouraging: a LinkedIn profile that hasn't been updated in three years, maybe a few random social media posts, and perhaps some photos from college that seemed funny at the time but less so when viewed by a potential employer.

That's not a brand. That's digital noise.

I once interviewed a candidate for a position. Impressive résumé. Strong recommendations. But out of habit, I Googled his name before the interview. The first result? A mugshot from a police arrest two years earlier.

The candidate didn't get the job. Not because of the arrest—people make mistakes—but because they hadn't managed their digital presence. They'd left their professional reputation to chance, and chance had not been kind.

Your online footprint is either intentional or accidental. There's no third option. And in an age where the first thing anyone does before meeting you is search your name, an accidental footprint is a professional liability.

LinkedIn gives you something rare: the ability to intentionally shape your digital identity, to define yourself before others define you, and to tell your story before the internet tells it for you.

From Commodity to Brand

Walk back into that supermarket. Look at those bottles of water.

Some are commodities, distinguished only by price. Others are brands, distinguished by story, by values, by the meaning they've built around a fundamentally identical product.

The water is the same. The perception is everything.

You have a choice. You can remain a highly skilled professional who competes on credentials and availability—functionally interchangeable with dozens or hundreds of people with similar backgrounds. Or you can build a brand that communicates your unique value, that extends beyond your current role, and that creates opportunities rather than waiting for them.

David Chen, the data scientist who kept getting passed over for promotion? After we worked together, he started sharing insights from his work—not bragging about results, but explaining methodologies, teaching concepts, and making complex techniques accessible. Six months later, he was getting invited to present to senior leadership. Twelve months later, he got the promotion. Not because he'd become better at data science, but because he'd become better at helping people understand what his data science could do for them.

He'd stopped being a commodity. He'd become a brand.

The question isn't whether you need a professional brand. In a world where expertise is abundant but clarity is scarce, where opportunities flow through networks you can't see, and where your next career move might come from someone who only knows you through your digital presence, you need a brand simply to be seen.

The question is: What will your brand say?

When people search your name, encounter your work, or hear about you from colleagues, what story will they find?

A title and a list of past positions?

Or a clear, compelling narrative about the value you create, the problems you solve, and the difference you make?

Because in the end, your brand isn't what you think about yourself. It's what others remember about you when you're not in the room.

And that memory—that persistent signal in a noisy world—is the difference between being a commodity and being recognized for what you actually are: irreplaceable.

3 Start Before You're Ready

The First Post

On a Sunday evening in March 2018, I sat at my kitchen table staring at a blank text box on LinkedIn. I'd written and deleted the same opening sentence four times. Each version felt wrong—too casual, too formal, too obvious, too obscure.

I was trying to share an insight from a meeting earlier that week, something about how experienced investors often make decisions based on pattern recognition rather than pure data analysis. It seemed worth sharing. But every time I started typing, a voice in my head would interrupt: *Who are you to write about this? Everyone already knows this. This isn't insightful enough. Wait until you have something better to say.*

I almost closed the browser.

Instead, I did something that felt reckless at the time: I posted it anyway. Not the polished version I imagined writing someday. Not the profound insight I hoped would eventually come. Just the unfinished thought I had that evening, expressed in simple sentences, with no grand conclusion.

Eleven people liked it. Eight of them I knew personally. Three were probably accidents.

That post changed nothing and everything.

It changed nothing about LinkedIn's algorithm or my professional reputation. But it changed everything about my relationship with the blank page. Because the next Sunday, when I sat down to write, the voice that said "wait until you're ready" was slightly quieter. And the Sunday after that, quieter still.

What I learned that evening, sitting at my kitchen table, wasn't about LinkedIn strategy or content creation. It was about something more fundamental: the gap between readiness and action, and why waiting for the former guarantees you'll never achieve the latter.

The Readiness Trap

In 2001, two psychologists at the University of California, James Prochaska and Carlo DiClemente, published research on what they called "stages of change." They were studying how people modify behavior—quitting smoking, starting exercise, changing careers—and they identified a predictable pattern.

Before anyone takes action, they go through a stage called "contemplation." They think about changing. They imagine what it would be like. They gather information. They wait for the right moment.

What Prochaska and DiClemente discovered was surprising: most people get stuck in contemplation. They think about starting for months, sometimes years, gathering more information, waiting for confidence to arrive, and preparing for a readiness that never quite materializes.

The people who actually change? They don't wait for readiness. They act before they feel prepared, and readiness emerges from the action itself.

This pattern shows up everywhere, but it's particularly acute in professional content creation. I've spoken with hundreds of professionals who want to start sharing insights on LinkedIn: smart people, experienced people, people with genuinely valuable perspectives.

And almost all of them are waiting for something:

More seniority. More confidence. The perfect first post. A better understanding of the platform. Something important enough to say.

They're stuck in contemplation, waiting for a signal that will never arrive, because readiness isn't a prerequisite for starting. It's a byproduct.

The First Post Paradox

Here's what nobody tells you about starting: your first post will not be your best post. It won't go viral. It probably won't even get much engagement. And that's exactly why you need to publish it.

Because the first post isn't about quality. It's about breaking the seal.

Think of it like this: Every professional content creator you admire—every thought leader whose posts you save, every writer whose insights you share—they all started with a first post that nobody remembers. Not because it was forgettable, but because it was necessary. It was the post that made the second post possible.

In his book *Atomic Habits*, James Clear describes what he calls "the two-minute rule": When you're trying to build a new habit, start with a version that takes two minutes or less. Not because two minutes is sufficient, but because two minutes is achievable. The goal isn't excellence; it's repetition. And repetition, over time, creates transformation.

Your first LinkedIn post is your two-minute rule. It doesn't need to be brilliant. It needs to be published. Because once it's published, something shifts. You're no longer someone who *intends* to share insights. You're someone who *does*.

That identity shift matters more than the post itself.

The Calendar Method

Let me tell you about a system that changed everything for me.

Every Saturday morning, I spend thirty minutes at a coffee shop with my phone and a notebook. While I'm waiting in line, I open my calendar and scroll through the previous week. Who did I meet? What did we discuss? What surprised me?

Then I scan my photos. Sometimes there's an image from a meeting, a conference, or a quiet moment that captures something worth exploring. I look through my saved articles, my email folders, and my voice notes.

I'm not looking for the perfect insight. I'm looking for a thread—something that made me pause during the week, something I'm still thinking about, something that might help someone else think differently.

Usually, I find two or three possibilities. I choose one. I write about it right there, in the coffee shop, often in a rushed scrawl in my notebook. Later, I'll refine it slightly, but the core always comes from that Saturday morning session.

This isn't about inspiration. It's about architecture. I've built a system that makes content creation inevitable rather than optional. The creativity happens within structure, not in opposition to it.

And here's what's interesting: over time, this practice changed how I experience my week. I started noticing insights I would have previously missed. A comment in a meeting would stick with me because I knew it might become a post. A pattern I observed would feel significant because I'd trained myself to look for patterns.

The system didn't just produce content. It transformed how I processed professional experience.

The Golden Hour

There's a concept in photography called the "golden hour"—that period shortly after sunrise or before sunset when the light is softest, warmest, and most forgiving. Photographers plan their shoots around the golden hour because the conditions are optimal.

Content creation needs a golden hour too. Not a time of day, but a protected space in your routine where creation becomes possible.

For me, it's Saturday morning at the coffee shop. For others, it's early morning before the household wakes up. Or late evening after the kids are asleep. Or lunch breaks at work.

The specific time matters less than the consistency. Your brain learns patterns. When you write at the same time, in the same context, with the same ritual, you lower the activation energy required to start. The habit becomes self-reinforcing.

Professional content creators talk about "writing rituals" as if they're mystical practices. They're not. They're simply behavioral psychology applied consistently. You're training your brain to associate specific contexts with creative output. Over time, showing up at your golden hour automatically triggers the mental state required for creation.

Treat it like a meeting with your future self. One you never skip. One that compounds value every time you honor it.

The Flow State

In 1975, a psychologist named Mihaly Csikszentmihalyi published research on what he called "flow"—that state of complete absorption where time disappears, effort feels effortless, and performance peaks.

Athletes call it "the zone." Musicians call it "being in the pocket." Writers call it finding their voice.

Csikszentmihalyi discovered that flow has prerequisites. It doesn't appear randomly. It emerges when challenge and skill are balanced—when a task is difficult enough to demand your attention but not so difficult that it triggers anxiety.

Here's what happens when you start posting consistently on LinkedIn:

In the beginning, there's no flow. The challenge overwhelms your skill. Every post feels like pushing a boulder uphill. You're hyper-aware of judgment, uncertainty, and imperfection.

But if you persist—if you push through the discomfort and maintain consistency—something shifts. The challenge remains, but your skill increases. The gap narrows. And at a certain point, usually around your twentieth or thirtieth post, you enter a new state.

Ideas start appearing everywhere. While you're showering, exercising, or commuting, your brain spontaneously generates content possibilities. You begin seeing potential posts in everyday conversations. The creative muscle, strengthened by repetition, starts working automatically.

You've found your flow.

And flow has a compound effect. The easier content creation becomes, the more you create. The more you create, the stronger the neural pathways. The stronger the pathways, the easier creation becomes. It's a positive feedback loop, and consistency is what initiates it.

The Compounding Insight

What I didn't understand that Sunday evening in 2018, sitting at my kitchen table, was that I wasn't just writing a post about investor decision-making. I was initiating a process that would compound over years.

That first post led to a second. The second made the third easier. By the tenth post, I'd started recognizing patterns in what resonated. By the fiftieth, I'd developed a voice. By the hundredth, I'd built an audience. By the two hundredth, opportunities were arriving that wouldn't have existed if I'd waited to feel ready.

None of this was visible in that first post. The value wasn't in the content—it was in the decision to publish despite uncertainty.

In economics, there's a concept called "option value"—the value of keeping opportunities open. Every time you post on LinkedIn, you're creating option value. You're making visible what you're thinking about, working on, and learning from. You're sending signals into a professional network that might connect you with opportunities you can't anticipate.

But option value only accrues when you take action. Waiting to feel ready, preparing for the perfect moment, gathering more confidence—none of these create option value. They're contemplation without action, intention without execution.

The professionals who succeed on LinkedIn aren't the ones who waited until they had something profound to say. They're the ones who started saying things and discovered profundity through practice.

The Permission You Don't Need

I want to tell you something that nobody told me: you don't need permission to share professional insights.

You don't need a certain job title. You don't need advanced degrees. You don't need your manager's approval. You don't need thousands of followers before you start.

You just need one insight, one observation, one lesson learned. And the courage to make it public despite the voice that says "wait until you're ready."

Because here's the truth about readiness: it's not a state you achieve before starting. It's a state that emerges from starting. Confidence follows action; it doesn't precede it.

Every professional content creator you admire went through the same progression you're about to go through. They wrote posts that felt inadequate. They hit publish with trembling hands. They checked notifications obsessively, hoping for validation. They questioned whether anyone cared.

But they kept going. Not because they were naturally confident or exceptionally talented. But because they understood that the gap between where they were and where they wanted to be could only be closed through repetition.

Your first post won't be perfect. Your tenth won't be perfect either. Perfection isn't the goal. Progress is the goal. And progress only happens when you start before you're ready.

The Invitation

So here's my invitation: Open LinkedIn right now. Think about one thing you learned this week. It doesn't need to be revolutionary. Just something that made you think differently, even for a moment.

Write three sentences about it. Not a polished essay. Just three sentences.

Post it.

Don't wait for confidence. Don't wait for the perfect insight. Don't wait until you've figured out your content strategy or developed your personal brand or learned the algorithm.

Start now. Start imperfect. Start uncertain.

Because six months from now, you'll look back at your first few posts and smile at how rough they were. But you'll also realize something profound: those imperfect posts were the most important ones you ever wrote.

Not because of their quality, but because they proved that starting was possible.

And once you know starting is possible, everything else becomes inevitable.

The only question is: Will you begin?

II Your Digital Storefront—Profile and Positioning

Your mindset is set. You're ready to start. But before you post a single word, you need a foundation that works for you 24/7. Your LinkedIn profile is that foundation. It's not a résumé—it's a landing page, a first impression, and a trust signal all in one. This section will show you how to build a profile that converts curiosity into connection, and how to position yourself so clearly that opportunities find you.

4 Building Your LinkedIn Landing Page: The Three-Second Test

The Recruiter Who Changed Everything

Every Monday morning at 9:00 AM, Lisa Wong opens her laptop at a WeWork in Toronto and starts what she calls "The Monday Scroll."

Lisa is a talent acquisition specialist at a mid-sized tech company. She's not at Google or Facebook. She doesn't have a fancy title or unlimited budget. She's just trying to fill roles before her manager starts sending "gentle reminder" emails.

Today, she needs to find a senior data analyst. The hiring manager gave her a shortlist of keywords: machine learning, Python, data visualization. "Someone who can translate technical work for non-technical stakeholders," he'd said. "And please, someone who actually updates their LinkedIn."

Lisa searches. Forty-seven profiles appear.

She starts clicking through them, one by one, coffee cooling beside her laptop.

Here's what Lisa doesn't tell the hiring managers: she spends about three seconds on each profile before deciding whether to keep reading or move on.

Not three minutes. Three seconds.

"I know it sounds harsh," she told me over video call last month. "But I'm looking at 40–50 profiles a day. If I spent five minutes on each one, I'd never leave my desk. So my brain just . . . filters."

In those three seconds, her brain is processing dozens of signals:

- Does this person look credible?

- Can they actually do what we need?

- Are they actively engaged in their field, or is this a ghost profile from 2019?

- Would my hiring manager be impressed if I sent this over?

Three unconscious questions. Three seconds to answer them.

If the answers are yes, she keeps reading. She looks at their experience, checks their recommendations, and scans their posts.

If not—or if anything feels off, unclear, or generic—she clicks the next profile.

Lisa isn't unusual. She's typical.

"Sometimes I feel guilty about it," she said. "Like I'm judging people too quickly. But then I remember: if someone can't make their profile clear in three seconds, how will they communicate complex ideas to our executives? That's literally what we need them to do."

Research backs up Lisa's instinct:

- 46% of people consider the headline the most important profile element (LinkedIn, 2024c)

- Most recruiters decide within six seconds whether a profile is worth reading (Jobvite, 2023)

- Profiles with professional photos receive 21× more profile views and 9× more connection requests (LinkedIn Groups Data, 2024)

Your LinkedIn profile isn't a résumé. It's a landing page.

A digital first impression that works 24/7, shaping how colleagues, clients, recruiters, and senior leaders perceive your credibility, your values, and your potential.

This chapter shows you how to build a profile that passes Lisa's three-second test—and turns those three seconds into three minutes, and those three minutes into opportunities you didn't even know existed.

The Three Invisible Checkpoints

Every visitor to your profile—whether they realize it or not—is unconsciously evaluating you through three checkpoints.

Lisa doesn't consciously think about these. They happen in her subconscious, in that three-second window before her brain decides "keep reading" or "next profile."

Checkpoint 1: Do I Trust This Person?

Trust signals come from:

- **Visual professionalism:** Photo quality, banner design, overall polish

- **Social proof:** Recommendations, endorsements, engagement on posts

- **Tonal authenticity:** Does this person sound real, or like corporate jargon generated by AI?

   What fails the trust test (Lisa's actual examples):

- Blurry photo cropped from a wedding or vacation

- Banner that's still LinkedIn's default blue

- About section that starts with "Results-oriented professional with extensive experience . . ."

- Last post from 2021 with zero activity since

- No recommendations, no endorsements, no evidence anyone vouches for them

"When I see these things, I think: this person doesn't take their professional presence seriously," Lisa said. "Why would we take them seriously?"

Checkpoint 2: Can They Help Me or Add Value?

Value signals come from **clarity** about:

- What you actually do (not just your job title)
- Who you serve or help
- What problems you solve
- What outcomes you deliver

What fails the value test:

- Generic headline: "Senior Analyst at [Company]"
- Vague About section that could apply to anyone
- No clear positioning or specialty
- Job description bullets copied from a résumé

"I need to know within seconds: can this person do what we need?" Lisa explained. "If I have to guess or dig through five paragraphs to figure it out, they're not getting a message from me."

Checkpoint 3: Are They Credible and Active?

Credibility signals come from **evidence:**

- Recommendations from people with real names and faces
- Featured work that showcases expertise
- Consistent activity (posts, comments, engagement)
- Current information (not abandoned in 2020)

What fails the credibility test:

- Profile last updated 3+ years ago
- Zero posts, zero comments, zero engagement

- Featured section empty or filled with irrelevant content

- Skills section with 50+ random skills (clear sign of "never pruned this")

"A profile from 2019 tells me this person isn't active on LinkedIn," Lisa said. "Which means they're probably not job hunting, not networking, not engaged in their field. So why would I waste a connection request?"

Your goal: all three answers should be "yes" within three seconds.

When they are, your LinkedIn profile becomes your 24/7 professional ambassador—working for you while you sleep, connecting you to opportunities you didn't even know existed.

The Banner: Your Visual Handshake

No one exchanges business cards anymore.

Your banner—that large rectangular image at the top of your profile—is the new handshake. It's the first thing people see, before they read a single word.

You have three seconds. Use them wisely.

Most people waste their banner on:

- ✖ Generic stock photos (a skyline, a handshake, abstract shapes)

- ✖ Their company logo alone

- ✖ Nothing at all (LinkedIn's default blue gradient)

"When I see the default LinkedIn banner, I know immediately: this person hasn't thought about how they're presenting themselves," Lisa said. "It's like showing up to an interview in pajamas. You might be qualified, but you're not taking this seriously."

What actually works:

A strong banner answers three questions in three seconds:

What do you do?

Not your job title—your function. Your purpose.

Not: "Chief Investment Officer"

But: "I help investors navigate market complexity with discipline and insight"

Not: "Senior Data Analyst"

But: "I turn messy data into clear decisions for non-technical teams"

Who do you help?

Be specific. Not "professionals" or "companies."

- Healthcare executives making budget decisions?

- Early-career engineers learning to code?

- Marketing teams trying to prove ROI?

The more specific, the more magnetic.

Why does it matter?

What's the outcome of your work?

- "Making calm, confident investment decisions in volatile markets"

- "Turning data into stories executives actually understand"

- "Building products people love without burning out teams"

Example of weak banner (Lisa sees this daily):

Generic stock photo of Toronto skyline at sunset. No text.

Signal to Lisa's brain: *"This person hasn't personalized their profile. Generic. Skip."*

Example of strong banner (Lisa saved this one):

Clean professional design with clear text overlay:

"Helping early-stage startups turn product ideas into market-ready launches"

Data PM | Ex-Shopify | Featured in TechCrunch, ProductHunt

Follow for product strategy insights

Signal to Lisa's brain: *"Oh. This person knows exactly who they are and what they do. Keep reading."*

See the difference?

The strong banner has three components:

PROMISE: One clear line capturing your professional purpose
   "Helping early-stage startups turn product ideas into market-ready launches"

PROOF: Recognition or achievement signaling credibility
   "Data PM | Ex-Shopify | Featured in TechCrunch, ProductHunt"

CALL TO ACTION: A simple nudge forward
   "Follow for product strategy insights"

Three elements. Three seconds. One clear impression.

For employees:

Your banner isn't about self-promotion. It's about alignment.

It should bridge your personal mission with your company's broader purpose.

Good example (corporate employee):

"Building financial literacy tools that help families make better money decisions | Product Manager @ [Fintech Company] | Follow for personal finance insights"

This works because:

- Clear purpose (financial literacy)

- Specific audience (families)

- Clear outcome (better decisions)

- Role mentioned but not emphasized

- Invitation to follow

Lisa's advice:

"Your banner is like the cover of a book. If it's boring or generic, I'm not opening it. But if it tells me in three seconds what you're about and why I should care, I'm in."

Tools for creating banners:

- Canva (free templates specifically for LinkedIn banners)

- Adobe Express (professional designs, user-friendly)

- Figma (if you want full design control)

Banner dimensions: 1,584 × 396 pixels

Investment: 30 minutes to create. Years of first impressions in return.

The Headline: Your One-Sentence Pitch

Your headline is the most powerful sentence on your profile.

According to LinkedIn research:

- 46% of respondents say the headline is the most important profile section

- Yet only 20% of users update theirs regularly

Most people waste it.

Common mistake (Lisa sees this 30+ times per day):

"Senior Data Analyst at ABC Company"

"That's not a headline," Lisa said, pulling up an example on her screen. "That's LinkedIn's auto-fill. It tells me your title, but it doesn't tell me what you actually DO or why it MATTERS."

The better formula:

What you do + How you're different + Who you help (or proof)

Example transformation:

Before: "Chief Investment Officer at XYZ Company"

After: "Chief Investment Officer | Translating economic trends into actionable investment insight | Read by 80,000+ professionals"

Why this works:

✓ **Expertise:** You understand economic trends

✓ **Differentiation:** You translate complexity into clarity (this is your unique angle)

✓ **Proof:** 80,000 people find your insights valuable (social proof)

The differentiation isn't vague:

✖ "Passionate"

✖ "Results-driven"

✖ "Strategic thinker"

✖ "Innovative"

These words mean nothing. Everyone claims them. They're LinkedIn's equivalent of "nice" on a dating profile.

Real differentiation is specific and provable:

✓ "Translating economic trends into actionable insight"

✓ "Making AI explainable for non-technical stakeholders"

✓ "Helping first-time managers lead without burning out"

✓ "Turning content into pipeline for B2B SaaS companies"

Lisa's real examples (profiles she actually contacted):

Example 1: Marketing Manager

Before: "Marketing Manager at Tech Startup"

After: "Marketing Manager | Helping B2B SaaS companies turn content into pipeline | 3× increase in qualified leads in 12 months"

Why Lisa contacted them:

> "The 3× increase was specific. It wasn't just a claim—it was a result. And 'content into pipeline' told me exactly what they specialize in."

Example 2: Data Scientist

Before: "Senior Data Scientist"

After: "Senior Data Scientist | Making AI explainable for executives who don't code | Featured speaker at Strata Data Conference"

Why Lisa contacted them:

"We needed someone who could translate technical work. This person literally led with that skill. Plus, the Strata mention showed credibility."

Example 3: HR Professional

Before: "HR Business Partner"

After: "HR Business Partner | Building cultures where people stay, grow, and do their best work | 15 years in tech scale-ups"

Why Lisa contacted them:

"The 'people stay, grow, and do their best work' line resonated. It wasn't HR jargon. It was human. And the 15 years in tech scale-ups matched what we needed."

See the pattern?

Before = Job title

After = Value proposition + proof or differentiation

Your headline should:

✓ Incorporate relevant keywords (for search optimization—recruiters search by skills)

✓ Immediately clarify what you do (for humans scanning quickly)

✓ Signal your unique value (for decision-makers evaluating you)

✓ Include proof when possible (numbers, recognition, outcomes)

When Lisa scrolls through forty-seven profiles:

- Headlines with value propositions get read
- Headlines with job titles only get skipped

"I know that sounds harsh," Lisa said. "But I'm not the only recruiter doing this. We all are. Your headline is your elevator pitch. Make it count."

Don't be skipped.

The About Section: Where Authenticity Lives (Or Dies)

This is where most profiles die.

"I can tell within the first sentence whether someone wrote their About section themselves or copied corporate jargon from their company website," Lisa said.

Common openings that make Lisa click "next profile":

✖ "I am a results-oriented professional with extensive experience in . . ."

✖ "Dynamic leader with a proven track record of . . ."

✖ "Passionate about leveraging synergies to drive innovation . . ."

✖ A bulleted list of skills and achievements (this is a résumé, not a profile)

"These openings are forgettable because they're interchangeable," Lisa explained. "They could describe anyone. And if it could describe anyone, it doesn't describe you."

Here's what actually works: Start with a story.

Not your entire career history. Not a list of accomplishments.

A moment. A belief. Something that shaped how you see the world.

Real example Lisa saved:

"I grew up in Mumbai watching my father interview candidates for his small manufacturing business. He'd spend hours with people—not just reviewing their degrees, but asking about their families, their struggles, their dreams. I remember being confused: 'Why does it take so long, Papa?' He said: 'Beta, anyone can read a résumé. I'm trying to see the person the résumé doesn't show.' Years later, I became a consultant helping companies hire talent. But that question—'Can you see the person the résumé doesn't show?'—is still what drives my work. How do we look beyond credentials to find potential?"

Why Lisa remembered this profile:

"The father. The Mumbai manufacturing office. The 'beta' detail—it was so specific, so visual. I could picture that conversation. And it wasn't about her achievements—it was about where her values came from. I wanted to keep reading."

Why storytelling works:

1. **It's human.** It shows the person behind the title.

2. **It's memorable.** You remember images and moments, not claims.

3. **It connects to purpose.** That early question still drives the work today.

Research shows:

- 85% of people read at least the first sentence **of an About section (LinkedIn, 2024)**
- Only 32% read the full section

That first sentence determines whether they keep reading or click away.

The structure that works:

STORY (one to two paragraphs):

A personal moment that shaped your approach. Make it specific, visual, relatable.

Don't write: "I've always been passionate about data."

Do write: "I discovered data analytics by accident. My college roommate was failing statistics, and I offered to help. While tutoring him, I realized I loved finding patterns in numbers—but I hated how complicated everyone made it. That tension—between complexity and clarity—became my career."

EXPERTISE (two to three paragraphs):

What you've done, how you've evolved, what you believe. But frame it as insight, not résumé bullets.

Don't write: "Managed 5 direct reports, delivered 15 projects, exceeded KPIs by 20%."

Do write: "Over the past eight years, I've helped teams at three different companies turn messy data into decisions executives trust. The biggest lesson? Technical accuracy matters, but storytelling matters more. If you can't explain your model to someone without a statistics degree, it won't get used."

VALUE PROPOSITION (one paragraph):

What you help others achieve. Who you serve. What problems you solve.

Don't write: "I specialize in data visualization and analytics."

Do write: "I help product teams understand their users without getting lost in dashboards. If you're trying to build data-informed products but drowning in metrics, I've probably solved that problem before."

INVITATION (one to two sentences):

A call to connect or collaborate. Make it easy and specific.

Don't write: "Feel free to connect."

Do write: "If you're building data products and want to talk through user research approaches, send me a message. I'm always up for a good data storytelling debate."

Complete example (Lisa's favorite from 2024):

"I accidentally became a product manager.

Fresh out of university, I took a customer support job at a startup because rent was due. Six months in, I'd logged 2,000 support tickets and noticed patterns no one else saw. Customers weren't asking for new features—they were struggling with features we'd already built but never explained properly.

I made a presentation. The CEO said, 'You should be in product, not support.' Two months later, I was.

That experience shaped everything. Good product management isn't about building more—it's about building right. Understanding what customers actually need, not what they say they want. Simplifying, not adding complexity.

Over the past six years, I've helped three companies launch products that people actually use (not just buy). The secret? Talk to customers before you build. Then talk to them again. Then talk to them some more.

I specialize in early-stage products where the biggest risk is building something no one needs. If you're trying to figure out what to build next—or whether what you built is working—let's talk."

Why this works:

✓ **Story:** The accidental career path (relatable, memorable)

✓ **Insight:** "Building right, not building more" (philosophy shown through story)

✓ **Expertise:** Six years, three companies, specific outcomes

✓ **Value proposition:** Early-stage products, reducing risk

✓ **Invitation:** Clear, specific, low-barrier

Lisa's advice:

"When someone reads your About section, they shouldn't just understand what you do. They should feel why it matters to you. That's the difference between information and connection."

Key principles:

✓ **Write in first person** (80%+ of users prefer this authentic voice)

✓ **Start with a hook** that addresses your audience's needs or shares a pivotal moment

✓ **Show expertise through stories**, not just claims

✓ **Include keywords naturally** for search optimization, but prioritize readability

✓ **End with a clear call to action** so people know how to engage

The About section isn't a résumé. It's a window into how you think.

When done right, it's the difference between being contacted and being ignored.

Visual Identity: The Elements That Reinforce Credibility

"Your banner and headline can be perfect," Lisa said, "but if your profile photo looks like a cropped vacation snapshot with a red Solo cup in the background, you've undermined everything."

Profile Photo Best Practices:

✓ **High-quality professional headshot** with good lighting

✓ **Neutral or branded background** (not a party, not a beach, not your kitchen)

✓ **Natural smile** (approachability matters—confident, not intimidating)

✓ **Professional attire** consistent with your industry

✓ **Recent photo** (not from 2015, not from your wedding)

✓ **Face fills 60% of frame** (too much background dilutes impact)

Research:

- Profiles with professional photos receive **21× more profile views** (LinkedIn, 2024)

- **9× more connection requests** (LinkedIn, 2024)

- **Faces with smiles** are rated as more approachable and trustworthy (Psychology Today, 2023)

"I know it sounds superficial," Lisa admitted. "But humans are visual. If I see a blurry photo, I assume you're not taking this seriously. If I see a professional photo, I assume you are. Fair or not, that's reality."

What Lisa actually sees (her real examples):

✘ **Cropped group photo** (half of someone else's shoulder visible)

✘ **Sunglasses photo** (can't see your face)

✘ **Gym selfie** (seriously)

✘ **LinkedIn's default silhouette** (instant skip)

✘ **Photo from 15 years ago** (when you meet in person, they won't recognize you)

☑ **Professional headshot, neutral background, natural smile, professional attire**

☑ **Consistent with how you look now**

☑ **Clear, high-resolution, well-lit**

Banner Image (1,584 × 396 pixels):

✓ **Reflect your personal brand** through colors and design

✓ **Include your tagline or value proposition**

✓ **Maintain visual consistency** with your overall brand

✓ **Update it** to reflect current focus or achievements

"Think of your banner and photo as a visual handshake," Lisa said. "They set the tone before anyone reads a word. Make them count."

Featured Section: Your Portfolio (Don't Waste This Space)

"This is prime real estate," Lisa explained, scrolling through a profile. "The Featured section is the first thing I see after your header. And most people leave it empty or fill it with random stuff from 2019."

Use it to showcase:

✓ **Key posts** that demonstrate your expertise

✓ **Articles or publications** you've written

✓ **Carousels or presentations** that got strong engagement

✓ **Media appearances** (podcasts, interviews, panels)

✓ **Projects or case studies** with measurable outcomes

✓ **Industry recognition** (awards, speaking engagements)

Quality over quantity.

"I'd rather see three really strong pieces of work than ten mediocre ones," Lisa said. "Show your best. Curate this section like you'd curate a gallery."

What Lisa looks for:

When she clicks on Featured content, she's answering one question:

"Is this person actively contributing to their field, or just claiming expertise?"

Evidence beats claims every time.

Real example (Lisa contacted this person):

Featured section included:

1. A post about data visualization best practices (300+ reactions, 50+ comments)

2. A presentation from a tech conference (slides showing clear expertise)

3. An article published on Medium about making data accessible (2,000+ views)

"Those three pieces told me: this person knows their stuff, they share their knowledge, and other people find them credible. That's exactly what we needed."

What NOT to feature:

✖ Certificate from a two-hour online course

✖ Generic company press release you had no role in

✖ Random post from 2019 with five likes

✖ Anything that doesn't showcase your expertise or credibility

Your Featured section should answer:

- What are you known for?

- What value do you add?

- Why should someone trust your expertise?

"If your Featured section is empty, you're missing a huge opportunity," Lisa said. "This is your chance to show, not just tell."

Skills, Endorsements, and Recommendations: Social Proof That Compounds

"I trust recommendations way more than skills endorsements," Lisa said. "Anyone can click 'endorse' in two seconds. But writing a recommendation? That takes effort. That's real."

Skills Section Best Practices:

✖ **Don't list fifty skills** (signals you never pruned this)

✓ **Prioritize five to ten key skills** that align with your positioning

✖ **Don't leave outdated or unrelated skills** (if "Microsoft Word" is your #3 skill in 2025, we have a problem)

✓ **Prune regularly** to keep your brand aligned

✖ **Don't hope for endorsements passively**

✓ **Strategically endorse others** for skills you genuinely see them demonstrate (often reciprocated)

"When I see someone with 50+ skills, I know they've never thought about positioning," Lisa explained. "When I see someone with 5–7 carefully chosen skills that match their headline and About section, I know they're intentional."

Recommendations: The Gold Standard

Recommendations are the strongest form of social proof on LinkedIn because they require:

- Time investment

- Public association

- Specific details

How to get meaningful recommendations:

1. Be specific in your request
   - ✗ **Don't say:** "Could you write me a LinkedIn recommendation?"
   - ✓ **Do say:** "I'm updating my LinkedIn profile and would really value your perspective on the supply chain project we worked on together. Would you be willing to write a brief recommendation highlighting how we collaborated and the outcome we achieved?"

2. Make it easy

   Offer to draft something they can edit if they're busy. Many people will appreciate this—just ensure it sounds like their voice, not yours.

3. Aim for diversity

   Get recommendations from:
   - Someone you **managed** (shows leadership)
   - Someone who **managed you** (shows coachability)
   - A **cross-functional partner** (shows collaboration)
   - A **client or external stakeholder** (shows impact)

Lisa's take:

"Profiles with 5+ quality recommendations are perceived as significantly more credible than those with none. When I see thoughtful recommendations from diverse sources, I think: other people vouch for this person. That matters."

What makes a recommendation valuable:

✓ **Specific examples** (not generic praise)

✓ **Measurable outcomes** when possible

✓ **Relationship context** (how they worked together)

✓ **Recent** (from the past two to three years)

Example of weak recommendation:

"John is great to work with. Highly recommend!"

Example of strong recommendation:

"I managed John for 18 months during our platform migration. His ability to translate technical complexity for executive stakeholders was exceptional—his presentations directly influenced our $2M budget approval. When challenges arose, he didn't hide problems; he came with solutions. Any team would be lucky to have him."

The difference?

Weak = generic, could apply to anyone

Strong = specific, credible, memorable

Activity: The Credibility Engine

"Your posts, comments, and shares are proof of life," Lisa said.

"They show you're active. Curious. Engaged. Thinking."

Even as an employee, a short reflection can position you as thoughtful:

✓ A lesson from a client conversation

✓ A takeaway from a book you read

✓ A framework you've developed

✓ A question you're wrestling with

✓ A congratulations to a colleague

Think of your content as an extension of your profile.

It signals you're not just present—you're participating.

Over time, that consistency compounds into authority.

Lisa's perspective:

"When I click on a profile and see someone who posted thoughtfully three days ago, I think: this person is active in their field.

When I see someone whose last post was in 2022, I think: this profile is abandoned. They're not job hunting, not networking, not engaged. So why would I reach out?"

You don't need to go viral.

You don't need thousands of likes.

You need to show up with value, repeatedly.

That's how trust is built:

- One post at a time

- One insight at a time

- One conversation at a time

Small actions, repeated consistently, create remarkable results.

The Call to Action: Making the Next Step Obvious

LinkedIn allows a "Call-to-Action" button on Premium profiles with options like "Book an Appointment" or "Let's Connect."

For employees, you might not need a booking link. But you should still **make the next step obvious**:

✓ "Follow for insights on [your expertise]"

✓ "Connect to discuss [specific topic]"

✓ "Read my weekly newsletter on [subject]"

✓ "DM me if you're working on [specific problem]"

The goal isn't to be clever. It's to remove friction.

When someone visits your profile and thinks, "I want more of this," your call to action should tell them exactly how to get it.

"So many profiles end with nothing," Lisa said. "I'm interested, I want to reach out, but I don't know if I should connect, follow, message, or what. Make it obvious."

5 Define Your Niche, Audience, and Value Proposition

The Problem of Looking Like Everyone Else

There's a data analyst named John Mitchell who spent six months trying to figure out why his LinkedIn posts weren't getting traction.

His content was solid. He posted about data visualization, analytics best practices, and insights from his work in NHS healthcare. But something wasn't working.

His posts averaged twelve likes, mostly from colleagues who felt obligated to support him. Profile views were flat. No one was reaching out to connect about his work.

He'd watch other analysts—some with less experience—get dozens of comments and connection requests, while his carefully crafted posts disappeared into the void.

"Maybe I'm just not interesting enough," he thought during his morning commute on the Tube, scrolling through yet another post of his that had gone nowhere.

Then he attended a conference in Manchester where a speaker asked the audience: "If I landed on your LinkedIn profile right now, could I tell you apart from the other fifty people with your job title?"

John's stomach sank. He already knew the answer.

He opened LinkedIn on his phone during the break and looked at his own profile with fresh eyes.

Headline: "Senior Data Analyst at [NHS Trust]"

About section: Started with "I am a data professional with 8 years of experience . . ."

Recent posts: Generic takes on data science trends

The answer was painfully clear: No. You couldn't tell him apart.

He looked identical to hundreds of other data analysts. Same vague language. Same generic positioning. Same invisible presence in a sea of sameness.

John closed his phone and sat with that realization for the rest of the conference. It stung. But it was also clarifying.

So he did something radical. He got specific.

He realized that what made him different wasn't that he worked with data—thousands of people do that. What made him different was that he specialized in making complex healthcare data understandable for clinical teams who don't speak statistics.

That night, back in his hotel room in Manchester, he rewrote his headline:

"Data Analyst | Translating complex NHS healthcare data into decisions that improve patient outcomes | Trusted by 15+ clinical teams"

He rewrote his About section to open with a story about a doctor at his Trust who made a critical treatment decision based on a visualization he'd created—and how that moment crystallized his purpose.

He refocused his posts to address one specific audience: NHS healthcare professionals who need to understand data but don't have technical backgrounds.

Three months later, John's posts were averaging 200+ engagements. He'd been invited to speak at two NHS healthcare conferences. A Medical Director at another Trust reached out about a leadership opportunity.

What changed? Not his expertise. Not his effort. Not the quality of his thinking.

What changed was clarity.

He stopped trying to be interesting to everyone and became invaluable to someone specific.

This is the power of positioning.

Why Positioning Matters (And Why Most People Skip It)

In the crowded professional space of LinkedIn, clarity is currency.

If people can't quickly understand who you are, who you serve, and how you add value, they move on. They have to—because they're looking at fifty other profiles that same day.

Most professionals skip positioning because it feels limiting.

"If I narrow my focus, won't I miss opportunities?"

"If I specialize, won't I seem less versatile?"

"If I define my niche too clearly, won't people think I can't do anything else?"

These are reasonable fears. They're also backward.

The paradox of positioning: The more specific you are, the more opportunities you create.

John worried that focusing on healthcare would make him less marketable. What actually happened: healthcare organizations started seeking him out specifically because he understood their world.

The data back this up:

Users with fully completed LinkedIn profiles are 40× more likely to receive opportunities than those with incomplete profiles. (LinkedIn Data)

Brand messages shared by employees achieve 561% greater reach than the same messages shared by official company accounts. (LinkedIn Marketing Solutions)

For employees, positioning defines how you move from being "someone in the company" to "someone people recognize and want to engage with."

Without clear positioning, your profile fades into the background.

With clear positioning, you become the person people think of when they have a specific need.

The Three Core Questions

To position yourself effectively, answer three fundamental questions:

Question 1: What Do I Do Best?

Not "What's my job title?" but "What do people come to me for?"

This isn't about being the world's leading expert. It's about identifying what you bring that others value.

How to find your answer:

Look at your track record:

- What problems do people regularly ask you to solve?

- What skills have you developed through repeated practice?

- What do colleagues compliment you on?

- What part of your job energizes you most?

- What unique perspective do you have based on your specific experience?

John's answer:

"I translate complex data into visual formats that non-technical people can understand and act on."

Not "I analyze data" (too generic).

Not "I'm good with numbers" (too vague).

But a specific capability he'd demonstrated dozens of times.

Question 2: Whom Do I Serve or Influence?

Define the audience that benefits most from what you bring.

This could be:

- Colleagues within your organization (specific departments or roles)
- Leaders and decision-makers (at what level?)
- Industry peers and professionals (in what sector?)
- Clients or customers (what type?)
- People at a certain career stage (early-career? mid-level? executives?)

The more specific, the more resonant.

"I help professionals" is vague and forgettable.

"I help mid-career professionals in financial services transition to leadership roles" is clear and magnetic.

John's answer:

"Clinical teams in healthcare settings—doctors, nurses, administrators—who need to make evidence-based decisions but don't have time to become data experts."

See how specific that is? That specificity is what made his visible.

Question 3: What Outcome Do I Deliver?

State the meaningful result or transformation you produce.

Don't focus on activities ("I analyze data," "I write code," "I manage projects").

Focus on outcomes ("I help teams make faster decisions," "I reduce deployment errors by 60%," "I deliver projects 20% under budget").

The difference:

Activity-focused: "I create data visualizations"

Outcome-focused: "I help clinical teams spot patterns that improve patient outcomes"

John's answer:

"I help healthcare professionals make confident, evidence-based decisions faster—without needing to become data experts themselves."

That's a transformation worth seeking out.

Your Value Proposition Formula

Together, these three answers form your value proposition:

"I help [audience] achieve [outcome] by [what you do]."

John's value proposition:

"I help clinical teams in healthcare settings make evidence-based decisions faster by translating complex data into visual insights they can understand at a glance."

More examples:

Generic: "I'm a project manager with strong communication skills."

Specific: "I help distributed engineering teams deliver complex projects on time by creating clarity when requirements get messy."

Generic: "I work in sustainability and ESG."

Specific: "I help corporate sustainability teams turn ESG data into compelling narratives that drive stakeholder action and regulatory compliance."

Generic: "I'm passionate about leadership development."

Specific: "I help first-time managers in tech companies transition from individual contributor to confident leader without burning out their teams."

See the pattern?

Generic = forgettable

Specific = memorable

Generic = invisible

Specific = searchable

Generic = applies to hundreds of people

Specific = applies to you

This clarity guides everything:

- Your content pillars
- Your profile language
- Your networking strategy
- Your conversation starters
- What opportunities you attract

The Venn Diagram of Positioning

Not every positioning is worth pursuing. Some look good on paper but won't sustain you.

Think of your positioning as the intersection of three circles:

Circle 1: Your Expertise
What you know deeply. Your professional skills, domain knowledge, accumulated wisdom.

Circle 2: Your Interest
What you care about. The topics that energize you, the problems you enjoy solving, the conversations you seek out.

Circle 3: Impact for Others
What your audience finds valuable. The needs, challenges, or aspirations of the people you want to reach.

Your sweet spot—your positioning—sits where all three overlap.

Why all three matter:

Expertise without Interest = Burnout
If you position yourself around something you're good at but don't care about, you'll hate creating content about it. You'll stop.

Interest without Expertise = No Credibility
If you position yourself around something you're passionate about but have no track record in, people won't trust you. You won't get opportunities.

Expertise + Interest without Impact = No Audience

If you position yourself around something you know and love but no one else cares about, you'll post into a void. No engagement. No opportunities.

The magic happens at the intersection.

John discovered this by accident:

Expertise: Data analysis, visualization, statistical interpretation

Interest: Making complex information accessible, helping people make better decisions

Impact: Healthcare professionals desperately needed data translated into actionable insights

All three circles overlapped perfectly.

If he'd positioned herself as a "data scientist who loves machine learning algorithms," he'd have expertise and interest—but his healthcare audience wouldn't care. They don't need ML; they need clarity.

If he'd positioned herself as "someone passionate about healthcare" without the data expertise, he'd have interest and potential impact—but no credibility.

The Venn diagram forced his to find the intersection that worked.

Testing Your Positioning

Once you've drafted your positioning, test it against four criteria:

Test 1: The Clarity Test

Can someone who doesn't know you understand what you do in one sentence?

If you have to explain it for three minutes, it's not clear enough.

John's positioning passes this test:

"I translate healthcare data into visualizations that clinical teams can act on."

One sentence. Anyone can understand it.

Test 2: The Differentiation Test

Could this positioning apply to anyone, or is it specific to you?

If twenty other people could claim the same positioning, it's too generic.

"Data analyst in healthcare" = Fails (hundreds of people)

"Data analyst who makes complex clinical data understandable for non-technical teams" = Passes (much smaller group)

Test 3: The Proof Test

Can you point to evidence (projects, experience, results) that backs up your positioning?

If you're positioning yourself as an expert in X, you should be able to cite three to five examples of doing X successfully.

John could point to:

- 15+ clinical teams he'd worked with

- Specific decisions made because of his visualizations

- Testimonials from doctors and administrators

- Presentations at healthcare conferences

That's proof.

Test 4: The Resonance Test

When you share this positioning with colleagues or peers, do they immediately nod and say, "Yes, that's exactly what you do"?

Or do they look confused and say, "Wait, I thought you did [something else]"?

John tested his positioning with three trusted colleagues. All three responded: "That's perfect. That's exactly what makes you valuable."

That's resonance.

If your positioning passes all four tests, you're ready to build content around it.

If it fails any test, refine it.

From Positioning to Content Pillars

Your positioning directly informs your content pillars—the three to five themes you'll post about consistently.

John's positioning:

"I help clinical teams make evidence-based decisions faster by translating complex healthcare data into visual insights."

His content pillars became:

Pillar 1: Data Visualization Best Practices

How to make data scannable, understandable, actionable

Pillar 2: Healthcare Decision-Making

Stories of how data influenced clinical decisions and outcomes

Pillar 3: Bridging Technical and Clinical Worlds

Lessons from working with doctors, nurses, administrators

Pillar 4: Career Development for Data Professionals

How he built his niche, what worked, what didn't

Each pillar supports his positioning. Each post reinforces who he is and who he serves.

This is why positioning matters: **it's the foundation everything else is built on.**

Without it, your content feels random:

- Monday: Data science trends

- Wednesday: Motivational quote

- Friday: Weekend plans

With it, every post becomes part of a coherent narrative:

- Every post serves your audience

- Every post reinforces your expertise

- Every post compounds your credibility

Random posting = invisible

Positioned posting = influential

The Evolution of Positioning

Here's what most people don't realize: positioning isn't permanent.

As your career evolves, your positioning should too.

Year 1–3: Junior Data Analyst

Positioning: "I help teams understand their data"

Year 4–7: Senior Data Analyst

Positioning: "I help healthcare teams make evidence-based decisions through data visualization"

Year 8+: Data Analytics Manager

Positioning: "I help organizations build data literacy so clinical teams can make confident decisions independently"

See the evolution?

Same core expertise (data → insights). But the scope expanded, the audience shifted, the outcome elevated.

When to revisit your positioning:

✓ **After a promotion** (responsibilities changed)

✓ **After developing a new skill** (capability expanded)

✓ **After discovering a passionate audience** (found your people)

✓ **Every twelve to eighteen months** (quarterly audit)

Red flags that your positioning needs updating:

- Your posts feel forced or boring to write

- Your engagement has plateaued or declined

- Opportunities you're getting don't match what you want

- You've outgrown your original niche

- People seem confused about what you do

When John eventually becomes a Director of Analytics, he'll need to adjust his positioning from "I translate data" to "I build teams and systems that translate data at scale."

Same foundation. Different altitude.

Practical Exercise: Define Your Positioning in Thirty Minutes

Grab a notebook. Work through these prompts:

Step 1: The Three Questions (ten minutes)

1. What do I do best? (Be specific. List three to five things people regularly come to you for)

2. Whom do I serve? (Be narrow. Describe your ideal audience in detail)

3. What outcome do I deliver? (Focus on transformation, not tasks)

Step 2: The Formula (five minutes)

Draft your value proposition:

"I help [audience] achieve [outcome] by [what you do]."

Write 3 versions. Pick the clearest one.

Step 3: The Venn Diagram (five minutes)

Draw three overlapping circles:

- Expertise (what you know)

- Interest (what you care about)

- Impact (what others value)

Where do all three intersect? That's your positioning sweet spot.

Step 4: The Four Tests (ten minutes)

Test your positioning against:

- Clarity: One sentence, anyone understands it?

- Differentiation: Specific to you, not generic?

- Proof: Can you cite three to five examples?

- Resonance: Would colleagues say "Yes, that's you"?

If it passes, you're done.

If it fails, refine and retest.

III Content Strategy— What to Say and How to Say It

You know what to say. Now let's master how to say it. This section builds your editorial framework—the content pillars that give your voice structure, the storytelling techniques that make your expertise memorable, and the psychological principles that make people stop scrolling and start reading. You'll learn what separates posts that get ignored from posts that get saved, and why the best content on LinkedIn doesn't try to go viral—it tries to be useful.

6 Building Your Content Pillars: Your Editorial Strategy

The Tale of Two Professionals

Six months into posting on LinkedIn, I couldn't figure out why one person's content captivated me while another's left me cold.

Both were senior professionals. Both posted regularly. Both had interesting insights.

Marcus Lim posted three times a week:

- Monday: Market analysis

- Wednesday: Motivational quote with sunset photo

- Friday: Weekend plans or personal celebration

- Random Tuesday: Book recommendation

- Occasional Thursday: Team appreciation post

After six months of following Marcus, I still couldn't tell you what he stood for. His feed was a collage without a theme. Each post existed in isolation, disconnected from the last, and unrelated to the next.

I'd see his name in my feed and think: "Oh, it's Marcus again. Wonder what random thing he's posting today."

Amit Gupta posted twice a week:

- Every post fell into one of three categories: investment philosophy, leadership lessons, or sustainability in finance

- Even when he shared personal stories, they connected to these themes

- After three months, I knew exactly what to expect—and I looked forward to it

- After six months, when someone mentioned sustainable investing, his name came to mind first

The difference between them wasn't frequency, quality, or effort.

The difference was **structure.**

Marcus was posting. Amit was **building.**

He had what Marcus lacked: **content pillars.**

What Are Content Pillars (And Why They're Not Optional)

A content pillar is a recurring theme that represents who you are and what you stand for professionally.

It's the intersection of three things:

- **Your expertise** (what you know)
- **Your values** (what you believe)
- **Your audience's needs** (what they care about)

Think of content pillars as the chapters of a book about your professional identity.

Each post is a page. Each pillar is a chapter. Together, they tell a coherent story about who you are and what you contribute.

Without pillars:

- Your posts feel random

- Your audience doesn't know what to expect from you

- You spend thirty minutes every post wondering "What should I write?"

- People remember individual posts but forget who wrote them

- Growth is slow and frustrating

With pillars:

- Your posts form a narrative

- Your audience develops expectations (the good kind)

- You rotate through pillars systematically

- People associate your name with specific topics

- Growth compounds because clarity creates recognition

This isn't just theory. It's math.

Research shows that consistent weekly posting results in 3× higher visibility compared to sporadic posting. But consistency without direction is just noise.

Content pillars give your consistency direction.

Why Most People Don't Use Pillars (And Why That's Their Loss)

Most professionals skip building content pillars because it feels limiting.

"If I focus on just three to five topics, won't I get bored?"

"What if something interesting happens outside my pillars?"

"Won't I seem one-dimensional?"

These fears are backward.

The Paradox of Pillars: Structure creates freedom, not constraints.

When Marcus sat down to post, he faced infinite possibilities. That paralysis meant he'd post whatever felt easy that day—a quote, a photo, a random thought.

When Amit sat down to post, he asked: "Which of my three pillars needs attention this week?" That constraint made the creative process easier, not harder.

He wasn't limited by his pillars. He was liberated by them.

Think about it: chefs don't cook randomly from every cuisine every day. They specialize. That specialization doesn't limit their creativity—it focuses it, deepens it, and makes them memorable.

Your content pillars do the same thing.

The Three Things Content Pillars Do for You

1. Build Authority Through Repetition

In 2006, psychologist Angela Duckworth began studying what separated high achievers from everyone else. His research eventually crystallized into the concept of **"grit"**—the combination of passion and perseverance.

But here's what often gets overlooked in his work: grit requires direction.

You can't persevere without knowing what you're persevering toward.

Content pillars are your direction. They're how you signal to your audience: "This is what I'm building expertise in. This is what I'm committed to understanding deeply."

When Amit posted about sustainable investing every other week for a year, something powerful happened: people started assuming he was an expert, even before they checked his credentials.

Repetition creates recognition. Recognition creates authority.

2. Stay Relevant to Your Audience

Your pillars should live at the intersection of what you know and what your audience cares about.

Marcus posted about topics he found interesting that day. Sometimes that aligned with what his audience needed. Often it didn't.

Amit posted about topics his audience was wrestling with, filtered through his expertise. Every post landed because it addressed a real need.

This is the difference between broadcasting and serving.

When your pillars are properly positioned, every post adds value to someone specific.

3. Reduce Creative Friction

Writer's block on LinkedIn isn't about lacking ideas. It's about lacking structure.

When you sit down to post and think "What should I write today?" you're starting from scratch every time. That's exhausting.

When you sit down to post and think "It's Tuesday, time for a leadership lesson" or "This week I'll share an industry insight," you're rotating through a system.

Amit maintained a simple rotation:

- **Week 1:** Investment philosophy

- **Week 2:** Leadership lesson

- **Week 3:** Sustainability insight

- **Repeat**

He rarely wondered what to post. The structure decided for his. All he had to do was pick the specific angle within that pillar.

That's the freedom of structure: it eliminates decision fatigue so you can focus on craft.

How to Find Your Content Pillars (A Twenty-Minute Exercise)

Finding your pillars isn't complicated. It just requires honest reflection.

Step 1: The Self-Audit (ten minutes)

Grab a notebook. Answer these questions:

1. **What topics light you up when you talk about them?**
   Not "should" or "professional obligation"—genuinely energize you.

2. **What problems do you solve at work every week?**
   The recurring challenges people come to you for.

3. **What do colleagues ask your advice about?**
   What expertise have others already recognized in you?

4. **What do you want to be known for three years from now?**
   Not where you are—where you're going.

5. **What unique perspective do you have based on your experience?**
   The intersection of your background that others don't share.

Step 2: The Triangle Test (five minutes)

Your pillars should live where three circles intersect:

Circle 1: Your Expertise (what you know deeply)

Circle 2: Your Interest (what you genuinely care about)

Circle 3: Audience Impact (what your audience needs)

Draw three overlapping circles. List potential topics in each circle.

Your content pillars are the topics that appear in **all three circles.**

Example:

Expertise: Financial analysis, risk management, market research

Interest: Sustainability, ethical investing, long-term thinking

Impact: Investors need clarity about ESG options

Pillar emerges: "Sustainable investing strategies for traditional portfolios"

Step 3: The Three-to-Five-Pillar Formula (five minutes)

Most professionals need **three to five content pillars:**

- **Three pillars** = Very focused, ideal if you have a tight niche

- **Four pillars** = Balanced, most common for employees

- **Five pillars** = Flexible, room for personal stories alongside expertise

More than five becomes scattered. Fewer than three becomes repetitive.

Amit's three pillars:

1. Investment Philosophy (expertise)

2. Leadership Lessons (personal growth)

3. Sustainability in Finance (purpose)

Example of four pillars for a product manager:

1. Product Strategy & Roadmapping

2. Cross-Functional Leadership

3. Customer-Centric Design

4. Career Development in Tech

Example of five pillars for an HR professional:

1. Talent Acquisition Best Practices

2. Building Inclusive Cultures

3. Employee Development & Retention

4. HR Analytics & Decision-Making

5. Personal Leadership Journey

See the pattern?

Three to four pillars focused on expertise

One to two pillars that humanize you (lessons, growth, values)

This balance makes you credible and relatable.

The Sandwich Theory: How to Rotate Your Pillars

In the 1970s, radio producers discovered something counterintuitive about audience engagement.

Playing hit after hit after hit didn't keep listeners tuned in. It exhausted them.

The solution became known as the Sandwich Theory:

- Open with a crowd favorite (hook attention)

- Slide in a slower track (create contrast, let audience breathe)

- Close with another hit (leave them wanting more)

The pattern worked because our brains don't crave relentless intensity. They crave rhythm.

The same principle applies to your content pillars.

Don't post the same pillar back-to-back-to-back. Rotate them to create rhythm and variety.

Amit's rotation (posting 2× per week):

Week 1:
- Post 1: Investment Philosophy

- Post 2: Leadership Lesson

Week 2:
- Post 1: Sustainability Insight

- Post 2: Investment Philosophy

Week 3:
- Post 1: Leadership Lesson

- Post 2: Sustainability Insight

Repeat.

This rhythm creates several benefits:

1. **Your audience never gets tired of one topic** (variety maintains interest)

2. **Each pillar gets regular attention** (consistency builds authority)

3. **You're never stuck** (always clear what comes next)

4. **Your brain stays engaged** (rotation prevents creative fatigue)

The Weekly Planning Trick:

Each weekend, look at your pillars and ask:

- "Which pillar haven't I posted about recently?"

- "What happened this week that connects to one of my pillars?"

- "Which pillar needs attention based on current events or audience questions?"

Pick the pillar. Then find the specific story or insight within it.

This is how Amit posted twice weekly for three years without burning out. The system decided what type of post. He only had to decide the specific angle.

Testing and Evolving Your Pillars

Not every pillar will resonate equally. That's valuable data.

The Ninety-Day Test:

Post across all your pillars for ninety days, then review:

Engagement Metrics:

- Which pillar gets the most meaningful comments?

- Which gets the most saves? (strongest signal of value)

- Which generates the most messages or opportunities?

Personal Metrics:

- Which pillar is easiest to write about?

- Which feels most authentic to your voice?

- Which connects most naturally to your daily work?

Audience Metrics:

- What are people asking follow-up questions about?

- What topics generate "This is so helpful!" responses?

- What content gets shared by your target audience?

After ninety days, adjust:

- **Pillar performing well + you enjoy it** = Keep it, expand it

- **Pillar performing well + you hate writing it** = Refine the angle or replace it

- **Pillar performing poorly + you love it** = Give it another ninety days with different angles

- **Pillar performing poorly + you don't enjoy it** = Replace it

Amit discovered this after six months:

His "Investment Philosophy" posts consistently outperformed everything else—high engagement, lots of saves, multiple opportunities traced back to them.

His "Leadership Lessons" posts got modest engagement but he loved writing them and they humanized his brand.

His original third pillar about "Market Analysis" felt generic and got minimal traction. After ninety days, he replaced it with "Sustainability in Finance"—where his unique perspective lived.

That adjustment transformed his presence. The new pillar resonated deeply, differentiated his from other financial professionals, and attracted his ideal audience.

Your pillars aren't set in stone. They're hypotheses you test with real content.

The Circle of Influence Test (What to Post, What to Skip)

Before you post, imagine three circles:

Inner Circle: Core Expertise

Topics directly related to your professional expertise. These are your primary pillars.

Post frequency: 60–70% of your content

Example for financial advisor: Investment strategies, risk management, portfolio construction

Middle Circle: Adjacent Topics

Topics that support or complement your expertise. These broaden your perspective without diluting your focus.

Post frequency: 20–30% of your content

Example for financial advisor: Communication skills, decision-making under uncertainty, building client relationships

Outer Circle: Tangential or Personal

Topics that may be interesting but aren't professionally relevant unless you can connect them meaningfully.

Post frequency: 0–10% of your content

Example for financial advisor: Weekend hiking trip (unless you connect it to a lesson about preparation, risk assessment, or long-term thinking)

The rule:

Post freely from the inner circle. Post selectively from the middle circle. Post rarely from the outer circle—and only when you can draw a clear professional insight.

This balance ensures you stay focused yet human.

Marcus violated this constantly—60% of his posts were outer circle content with no professional connection. His audience never knew whether he was a finance professional or a lifestyle influencer.

Amit maintained discipline—70% inner circle, 25% middle circle, 5% outer circle (and always with a professional lesson attached).

His focus built authority. His selective personal content maintained humanity.

The Niche-to-General Bridge

Here's a powerful principle from sociology:

In 1973, Mark Granovetter published "The Strength of Weak Ties." He discovered that people don't get jobs through their closest friends. They get them through acquaintances—through loose connections in their network.

The same principle applies to content:

Your niche content (strong ties) builds credibility.

Your general insights (weak ties) expand reach.

The magic happens when you bridge both:

Example: Start niche, expand to universal

Niche post: "When analyzing emerging market bonds, I always stress-test against three currency scenarios . . ."

Bridge to universal: "This taught me something about decision-making under uncertainty: the best choices aren't about predicting the future—they're about preparing for multiple futures."

The niche establishes expertise. The universal insight creates relatability.

Amit mastered this:

His posts about sustainable investing were niche—but he always found the universal lesson:

- "Sustainable investing isn't just about returns. It's about what we're building toward."

- "ESG analysis taught me that the best long-term investments are those that serve both profit and purpose."

The niche attracted his target audience (institutional investors interested in sustainability).

The universal insight made his shareable beyond that niche (anyone interested in purpose-driven work).

This is how you build authority in your field while remaining relevant to broader audiences.

Common Pillar Mistakes (And How to Avoid Them)

Mistake 1: Too Many Pillars

"I want to cover finance, leadership, productivity, fitness, travel, and parenting."

Problem: You become a generalist in everything, an expert in nothing.

Solution: Pick three to five that matter most to your professional identity. You can still occasionally post about other topics—just don't make them pillars.

Mistake 2: Too Similar Pillars

"My three pillars are: data analysis, data visualization, and data storytelling."

Problem: These are basically the same thing. Your audience won't notice variation.

Solution: Make pillars distinct. Instead: Data Strategy, Cross-Functional Collaboration, Career Growth in Analytics.

Mistake 3: Pillars You Don't Care About

"I should post about AI because everyone's talking about it."

Problem: You'll burn out writing about topics that don't genuinely interest you.

Solution: Only build pillars around topics that energize you. Authenticity is mandatory for longevity.

Mistake 4: No Personal Pillar

"All four of my pillars are technical expertise."

Problem: You'll seem one-dimensional. People connect with humans, not expertise robots.

Solution: Include at least one pillar that reveals your humanity—lessons learned, growth journey, values, or reflections.

From Activity to Identity

Marcus posted for 18 months. He gained 400 followers. His engagement averaged 15 likes per post. No opportunities came from LinkedIn.

Six months in, he'd started to feel discouraged. "I'm putting in the work," he told a colleague over lunch. "But nothing's happening. Maybe LinkedIn just doesn't work for people like me."

He kept posting—but without direction, each post felt like starting over. By month 18, he was exhausted and ready to quit.

Amit posted for 18 months. He gained 5,200 followers. His engagement averaged 180 reactions and 15–20 meaningful comments per post. He received 7 speaking invitations, 3 consulting inquiries, and 1 job offer that led to a significant career move.

When a friend asked his secret, he smiled. "I stopped posting whatever came to mind and started posting what I stand for. Three pillars. That's it. Once I had that structure, everything got easier."

Same time investment. Dramatically different outcomes.

The difference wasn't talent, luck, or effort.

The difference was structure.

Marcus posted activity—disconnected thoughts that never accumulated into anything memorable.

Amit posted identity—a coherent narrative about who he was and what he stood for.

His content pillars transformed activity into identity.

And identity is what builds trust, recognition, and opportunity.

Two years later, Marcus discovered content pillars. He restructured his presence around three themes: fintech innovation, risk management, and career transitions.

Within six months, his engagement tripled. Within a year, he received his first speaking invitation.

"I wasted 18 months figuring out what Amit knew from day one," he told me. "Structure isn't limiting. It's liberating."

He was right.

His content pillars transformed activity into identity.

And identity is what builds trust, recognition, and opportunity.

Your Action Plan: Build Your Pillars This Week

Monday: The Reflection (twenty minutes)

Answer the five self-audit questions. Identify five to seven potential topics.

Tuesday: The Triangle Test (fifteen minutes)

Draw the three circles (Expertise, Interest, Impact). Map your topics. Find the intersections.

Wednesday: Select Your Three to Five Pillars (fifteen minutes)

Choose the topics that passed the triangle test. Ensure they're distinct and balanced (expertise + human).

Thursday: Create Your Rotation (ten minutes)

Map out a four-week posting schedule showing how you'll rotate through pillars.

Friday: Write Your First Pillar Post (thirty minutes)

Pick your strongest pillar. Write one post. Publish it.

Total time investment: ninety minutes.

By Friday, you'll have clarity about what you'll post for the next year.

That clarity is what separates professionals who post from professionals who build.

7 What to Post (And What Not to Post)

The Economist Got It Right (And Wrong)

In October 2025, *The Economist* published an article titled "LinkedIn and the art of self-promotion." The subtitle captured the tension perfectly:

"Everyone does it. It's still appalling."

The article opened with a caricature: "*Bryan Follicle, Thought Leader, Serial Founder, Dad, Husband, Son*"—a satirical persona that exaggerates the overly-branded LinkedIn profiles we've all scrolled past.

The kind of profile where every post begins with "Humbled to announce . . ." or "Grateful for this incredible journey . . ." or "Thrilled to share . . ." The kind where achievement announcements read like press releases written by someone's publicist rather than a human being.

The Economist's diagnosis was accurate:

Self-promotion on LinkedIn has become unavoidable. In a competitive professional market, visibility isn't optional—it's strategic. The platforms reward signals: post metrics, endorsements, follower counts, and engagement rates.

Everyone is marketing themselves, cloaked in humility ("I'm humbled . . .") or gratitude ("So grateful . . ."), but marketing nonetheless.

The article observed that while self-promotion has become practically necessary, the form it takes often lacks sincerity. Platforms like LinkedIn incentivize visible signals, pushing users toward more visible self-promotion. The human instinct is modesty, but the algorithm rewards visibility.

But here's where The Economist stopped short:

They captured the problem but missed the solution.

The issue isn't that self-promotion exists. The issue is that most people are doing it badly.

They're announcing *what happened to them* instead of sharing *what they learned that could help others.*

They're saying "Look at me" when they should be saying "Look at what I discovered."

The article was right: when self-promotion becomes performative—when someone's entire LinkedIn presence reads like a series of staged achievements and curated milestones—we cringe. It's appalling.

But the article missed this: there's a form of self-promotion that doesn't feel like promotion at all.

It feels like contribution.

When you shift from announcement to insight—from "I did this" to "Here's what this taught me"—you're not self-promoting. You're value-sharing.

That's the difference between Bryan Follicle, Thought Leader™, and someone people actually want to hear from.

This chapter shows you how to make that shift.

The Mistake I Made for Two Years

In the early days of my LinkedIn journey, I made a curious mistake.

I posted things like: "I'm humbled to speak at this event." Or "Honoured to be part of this amazing panel."

Many of us have done this. It feels polite. Professional. Safe.

But here's what I didn't realize: those posts were adding virtually no value.

They announced what I did, but not what I learned. They showed where I'd been, but not what I saw. And in the economy of attention that is LinkedIn, that's a fatal flaw.

When every post sounds the same (humbled, honored, grateful), people scroll past. Not because the sentiment is insincere, but because it's indistinguishable from everyone else's.

The truth is, you don't build thought leadership by announcing milestones. You build it by sharing insights.

The Economist was right about the symptom: self-promotion has become ubiquitous and often appalling.

This chapter gives you the cure.

The Announcement Trap

Consider this: why do milestone announcements fail?

It's not that people don't care about your achievements. It's that announcements are fundamentally self-referential. They start and end with you.

The most powerful posts, by contrast, don't start with you at all. They start with a thought. An observation. A pattern you've noticed that others have missed.

Something that makes people say, "I never looked at it that way before."

That's how you add value: by showing a perspective, a framework, or an idea that helps someone else think differently.

It doesn't have to be complicated.

It just has to be yours.

When I speak at an event today, I don't post about being humbled or grateful. I post about the one thing I learned that day. The conversation that changed my view. The insight that challenged me. The data that surprised me.

That's what people come to LinkedIn for: to learn, reflect, and grow.

Why Generic Content Fails

The internet is full of generic lessons that sound good but say little.

"Be resilient." "Never give up." "Believe in yourself."

These aren't insights. They're platitudes.

In his book *Made to Stick*, Chip Heath describes what he calls the "Curse of Knowledge." Once we know something, we find it nearly impossible to imagine what it's like not to know it. The result? We resort to abstract generalizations instead of concrete specifics.

Generic content suffers from the same curse. It doesn't tell people who you are, what you've learned, or how you think.

On LinkedIn, generic content blends into the background. It doesn't offend anyone, but it doesn't move anyone either.

And when everything you post could have been written by anyone, you lose your voice.

The antidote to generic content is specific content.

Not "Leadership is about listening."

But "Last Tuesday, I interrupted my team member three times in one meeting. The fourth time I started to speak, I caught myself. I stayed quiet. What she said next changed our entire project direction. Here's what I learned about the cost of not listening."

See the difference?

One is a platitude anyone could write. The other is a story only you can tell.

Shock Posts Don't Work for Employees

Every platform has its provocateurs.

The voices who thrive on controversy and attention. They post with sharp edges, using bold or polarizing opinions to spark outrage, debate, and clicks.

On social media, that strategy can work. It drives engagement. It feeds the algorithm.

But on LinkedIn, it rarely builds credibility.

For employees, shock content isn't just risky. It's self-defeating.

When you're part of an organization, your professional identity is intertwined with your company's brand. You're not just representing yourself. You're representing the values and culture of your workplace.

A post designed to "stir things up" might go viral, but it can also raise quiet questions internally: Is this person aligned with our tone? Can they be trusted to speak for us?

The Provocateur Paradox

Early in my LinkedIn journey, I used to follow people who built their audience by being deliberately provocative.

They were entertaining, sometimes even brave, for saying what others wouldn't. For a while, I thought they were the ones making LinkedIn interesting, breaking the monotony of corporate language.

But over time, I noticed something else.

Their posts generated reactions, not relationships.

The attention they gained was fleeting. The respect they lost was lasting.

In the 1960s, psychologist Leon Festinger developed what he called "social comparison theory." He discovered that people constantly evaluate themselves by comparing themselves to others. But here's the interesting part: we don't compare ourselves to everyone. We compare ourselves to people we consider similar to us—people in our peer group.

On LinkedIn, when an employee posts provocative content, their peers (colleagues, industry professionals, and potential collaborators) begin a subconscious evaluation:

"Would I say that? Would I want to work with someone who says that?"

The answer often determines whether credibility grows or shrinks.

What Sustains a Voice

What sustains a voice on LinkedIn isn't controversy. It's credibility.

People remember those who bring clarity, not chaos. Those who challenge ideas with substance, not sarcasm. Those who make others think, not fight.

If you're an employee, your most powerful posts aren't the ones that make people argue. They're the ones that make people pause. The ones that show reflection, humility, and perspective.

There's a difference between being bold and being reckless.

Boldness is having the courage to share truth with empathy and evidence.

Recklessness is sharing for attention.

The first builds influence. The second burns bridges.

Consider the case of two professionals I followed early on. Both had strong opinions about industry trends. Both posted regularly.

The first would write things like: "Anyone still doing X is a fool. Change my mind."

The second would write: "I used to believe X. Here's what changed my thinking."

The first got immediate engagement: angry comments, defensive responses, shares from people who enjoyed the drama.

The second got something else: thoughtful replies, private messages from senior leaders, speaking invitations, job offers.

Five years later:

The first had a large following but limited professional opportunities.

The second had built a career partly on the strength of their LinkedIn voice.

The Heat Versus Light Principle

LinkedIn doesn't reward outrage. It rewards insight.

And the voices that endure are those that add light, not heat.

Voices that make people want to listen again.

The Economist noted that the best self-promotion shifts from *"look at me"* to *"look at what I deliver / how I help / why this matters."*

That's exactly right.

When you move from announcement to contribution, from headline to impact, self-promotion stops feeling appalling—because it stops being about self.

What to Post Instead

So what should you post?

Here's the principle that changed everything for me:

Post what only you can say.

It's the simplest rule, but also the hardest to follow.

Not what sounds impressive. Not what everyone else is posting. Not what you think LinkedIn "wants."

What only you—with your specific experiences, perspectives, and lessons—can offer.

That could be:

- ✓ A story from your work that taught you something nobody mentioned in the meeting
- ✓ A question you're wrestling with (not one you've already answered)
- ✓ A framework you've developed through trial and error, not borrowed from a book
- ✓ A connection you've made between your world and a larger trend others haven't noticed

Here's what surprises most people: the best stories rarely come from your biggest wins.

They come from the small, almost ordinary moments that shaped who you became.

The mentor who said one sentence that changed your trajectory. The quiet decision you made in a bathroom mirror before a presentation. The day you finally spoke up after staying silent for three years.

These are the moments that create connection.

They reveal authenticity without announcing it. They show growth without claiming arrival. They express gratitude without performing it.

On LinkedIn, these small moments of truth resonate more than any announcement ever could.

The lesson you extracted from failure. The insight that shifted your thinking. The thank-you you never said out loud but wish you had.

Because people don't just follow success. They follow sincerity.

When you share something that reveals how you think—not just what you've achieved—you stand out in a sea of identical announcements.

Insight doesn't come from repeating what others have said. It comes from noticing what others have missed.

The Art of Sharing Without Showing Off

Confidence is magnetic. Arrogance is repellent.

On LinkedIn, that line can be thinner than you think.

A post meant to celebrate can easily sound like chest-thumping. What begins as gratitude can slip into grandstanding. And while it's natural to feel proud of achievements, remember this: humility, not hype, builds trust.

The Economist captured this tension perfectly: the problem isn't that self-promotion exists—it's that most of it reads as performative rather than authentic. Their "Bryan Follicle, Thought Leader™" caricature exaggerates what happens when someone's LinkedIn becomes a series of announcements rather than contributions.

There's nothing wrong with sharing milestones.

But the difference between connection and alienation lives entirely in how you share them.

A simple shift in focus—from me to we, from achievement to insight, from what happened to what it taught you—changes everything.

When You Win an Award

Instead of announcing, "Humbled to receive this award," use that moment to illuminate someone else.

Name the mentor who gave you your first real chance. Acknowledge the mistake you made that taught you what this award now recognizes. Share the moment of doubt that almost stopped you from trying.

That transforms a self-congratulatory post into a story. One that teaches, inspires, and connects.

Consider the difference:

Version A:

"Humbled to receive the Industry Leadership Award. Thank you to everyone who supported me on this journey."

Version B:

"This award sits on my desk now, but I keep thinking about Sarah. She was my first manager. I was 23, overconfident, and catastrophically inexperienced. I made every rookie mistake in the handbook—some twice. She could have written me off. Instead, she stayed late one Tuesday to show me how to actually read a P&L. Not because it was her job. Because she believed I could learn. This one's for her."

Version B tells us something Version A never could: who you are, what shaped you, and why character matters more than credentials.

When You Speak on a Panel

It's tempting to summarize your own brilliant points and share a photo of yourself on stage.

But the more powerful move? Spotlight what others said.

The perspective that challenged your assumptions. The data point that made you rethink your position. The question from the audience that you're still pondering three days later.

By elevating others, you earn credibility without claiming it.

When You Join a Board or Start a New Role

Don't announce the position. Illuminate the mission.

What does this organization stand for that matters to you personally? Why does this work need to exist in the world? How does it connect to something you've always cared about?

Let the story of the cause take center stage. Let your role emerge as a natural consequence of that story.

When people see purpose behind your involvement, they don't see self-promotion. They see alignment.

When You Meet a VIP or Public Figure

It's easy to post a photo and say, "An honor to meet [name]."

That's fine. It's also forgettable.

The deeper post shares **why** you've always admired them. Not their fame—the specific thing they said or did that influenced your thinking. The lesson you took from ten minutes in their presence. The question you asked and the answer that surprised you.

Turn a celebrity encounter into a human moment, and people remember it.

The Litmus Test

Before I post anything, I ask myself one question:

"Could anyone else write this, or could only I write this?"

If it sounds like a Mad Libs template anyone could fill in, I don't post it.

If it reflects my specific perspective, experience, or hard-won lesson, I do.

That's the filter that keeps content authentic and useful.

That's what separates signal from noise.

The Economist identified the symptom: most LinkedIn self-promotion is appalling because it's performative.

This chapter gave you the cure: shift from announcement to insight, from "look at me" to "look at what I learned."

The filter that separates authentic contribution from appalling self-promotion is simple:

Does this post add value to someone else's thinking, or does it just announce my achievement?

If it's the former, post it with confidence.

If it's the latter, rewrite it until it is.

That's how you avoid becoming Bryan Follicle, Thought Leader™.

That's how you build a voice people actually want to hear.

8 The Art of Storytelling for Employees

The Post That Changed Everything

In March 2022, Priya Sharma sat in her car in the basement parking lot of her client's office building in Lower Parel, Mumbai.

The meeting had just ended. The Mumbai heat was already building, even underground—the AC hummed, but she barely noticed.

She'd just presented what she thought was a brilliant solution—backed by data, thoroughly researched, perfectly structured. Three weeks of work. Late nights at her Andheri apartment, reviewing financial models until 2 AM. Multiple revisions. Her manager had approved it. Her team thought it was solid.

When she finished, the client—a senior VP at one of Mumbai's largest BFSI companies—sat back and said:

"This is impressive work. But it doesn't solve our actual problem."

Priya had spent three weeks building the wrong thing.

She sat there for ten minutes, watching other cars exit the parking garage, replaying every conversation. The honking of Mumbai traffic above felt distant. The usual chaos of Lower Parel's streets—autorickshaws weaving between cars, street vendors calling out, the perpetual construction noise—all of it faded.

How had she missed this?

She'd been so focused on showcasing her expertise—proving she deserved to be in that room as a consultant in Mumbai's competitive corporate landscape, proving her technical capabilities were as sharp as anyone's—that she'd stopped listening to what they actually needed.

The drive back to her office in Powai took ninety minutes in traffic. Ninety minutes of replaying every meeting, every email, every assumption she'd made.

That night, she wrote about it on LinkedIn.

She drafted it at 11 PM, sitting at her kitchen table in Andheri. Deleted it. Rewrote it. Deleted it again.

In Indian corporate culture, you don't usually admit mistakes so publicly. You don't show vulnerability. You show competence, confidence, and credentials. You prove you belong.

But something made her hit publish anyway.

The post wasn't about a major achievement. It wasn't announcing a promotion or celebrating a milestone.

It was about the moment she realized she'd been doing her job all wrong.

She wrote about that client meeting. About the walk back to her car after the presentation. How she sat in the driver's seat replaying every conversation she'd had with the client. How she realized she'd been so focused on showcasing her expertise that she'd stopped listening to what they actually needed.

That post—about professional humility, about the difference between being impressive and being useful—got 847 comments.

People didn't just like it. They felt it.

They shared their own stories of similar moments. Senior professionals from across India commented about times they'd made the same mistake. Junior colleagues thanked her for being honest about something everyone experiences but rarely admits.

Comments came from Bangalore, Delhi, Pune, and Chennai. From consultants, bankers, engineers, product managers. From professionals across Southeast Asia who'd felt the same pressure to prove themselves.

Three months later, Priya was invited to speak at an industry conference in Bangalore.

Not because of her technical expertise, but because people remembered her story.

The invitation email said: "We want someone who can connect with our audience, not just inform them. Your LinkedIn presence shows you can do that."

Here's what Priya understood that most professionals miss:

Facts tell. Stories sell. But on LinkedIn, stories do something more powerful—they connect.

They turn expertise into emotion. Information into inspiration. Credentials into credibility.

And for employees, storytelling isn't about performance. It's about presence. It's how you make your professional journey visible, relatable, and human.

Why Most Employee Posts Fall Flat

When employees post on LinkedIn, most default to one of two extremes:

Extreme 1: The Corporate Press Release

"Excited to announce that our team successfully completed the Q3 initiative ahead of schedule. Grateful for the opportunity to work with such talented colleagues. Proud of what we've accomplished together."

Polished. Professional. Perfectly forgettable.

There's no story here. No humanity. No reason to care beyond polite support from colleagues who feel obligated to like it.

Extreme 2: The Overshare

"Just had the worst day. My manager doesn't appreciate me. Thinking about quitting. Anyone else feel like corporate life is soul-crushing?"

Too personal. No professional context. Creates discomfort, not connection.

True storytelling sits in the middle.

It blends authenticity with intention. Vulnerability with purpose. Personal experience with professional insight.

The formula:

1. **Start with a human moment** (scene, emotion, challenge)

2. **Extract the professional lesson** (insight, shift in thinking)

3. **Invite reflection** (make it relevant to your audience)

Priya's post worked because it hit this balance perfectly:

✓ **Human moment:** The realization that she'd built the wrong solution by not truly listening

✓ **Professional lesson:** How she changed her approach from showcasing expertise to understanding needs

✓ **Invitation:** "When have you realized you were solving the wrong problem?"

Personal enough to be memorable. Professional enough to be valuable. Universal enough to resonate.

Priya's reflection:

"I was terrified to post it," she told a colleague over chai at a Powai café weeks later. "In Indian corporate culture, especially in consulting, you're supposed to project confidence. You don't admit you got it wrong. But that's exactly why I posted it—because I knew others felt the same pressure and never talked about it."

The Science of Why Stories Work

In the early 2000s, Chip Heath, a Stanford business professor, began studying what makes ideas stick.

He and his brother Dan analyzed thousands of messages: advertising campaigns, urban legends, corporate communications, and public health warnings. They wanted to understand why some ideas spread while others died on arrival.

What they discovered surprised them:

The most memorable ideas weren't the most factual. They were the most human.

Ideas wrapped in stories. Grounded in emotion. Connected to real experiences.

Facts informed. Stories transformed.

For employees on LinkedIn, this matters more than you might think.

When you post: "Our team improved efficiency by 23% this quarter," people scroll past. It's a fact. It's impressive. It's also interchangeable with a hundred similar facts.

But when you post: "Three months ago, our process was so inefficient that our best analyst quit out of frustration. That resignation forced us to completely rethink how we worked. Here's what we learned . . ." people stop scrolling.

The 23% improvement becomes meaningful because there's a story behind it.

The story shows:

✓ The human cost of inefficiency (analyst quits)

✓ The wake-up call (forced to rethink)

✓ The transformation (what we learned)

Stories don't just convey information. They make you feel the stakes.

And feeling the stakes is what makes people remember—and engage.

Priya's discovery:

After her post went viral, she analyzed what resonated. "It wasn't the fact that I made a mistake," she said. "Everyone makes mistakes. It was that I showed the internal dialogue—the moment in the car, the replaying of conversations, the realization. That's what people connected with. They'd been in that car too."

The Employee Advantage (Why Your Stories Matter More)

Employees often underestimate their storytelling power.

They think they need a title, a platform, or a PR team to have stories worth telling.

But the truth is: employees are the most credible storytellers a company has.

In 2012, the **Edelman Trust Barometer**—an annual survey measuring public trust in institutions—revealed something striking:

When asked who they trusted most to tell the truth about a company:

- **CEOs:** 38%

- **Regular employees:** 52%

People trust employees fourteen percentage points more than they trust executives.

Not because employees know more. But because they seem more real. They're perceived as having less to gain from spinning the truth.

When a CEO posts "Our company values innovation," it sounds like marketing.

When an employee posts "Last week, my manager gave me permission to try a new approach that failed—and then helped me figure out what to do next," it sounds like evidence.

Your stories bring the brand to life.

You show:

✓ **Culture in action** (not just claimed values)

✓ **How values translate into behavior**

✓ **How purpose translates into daily decisions**

✓ **What it's actually like to work there**

The best company storytelling doesn't come from marketing departments. It comes from employees who write with sincerity about what they learn, why they care, and how they grow.

This is your advantage. Use it.

What happened to Priya:

Three companies reached out to her after that post—not to hire her as a consultant, but to ask if she'd be willing to speak to their teams about client listening and professional humility.

"They didn't see me as a consultant who made a mistake," Priya said. "They saw me as someone who could teach what most consultants never admit: that expertise without listening is just noise."

What Makes a Good LinkedIn Story

A powerful story doesn't need drama. It needs three things: clarity, emotion, and a lesson.

Think of it as a simple flow:

THE SCENE (Where It Happened)

Something specific that made you think. A meeting, a mistake, a client insight, a piece of feedback, a moment of realization.

THE EMOTION (What You Felt)

The human moment. The struggle. The uncertainty. The surprise. What changed in your thinking.

THE INSIGHT (What You Learned)

The shift in perspective. The takeaway. The lesson worth sharing.

THE REFLECTION (What It Means)

The invitation for others to connect it to their experience. The question that opens dialogue.

Most great LinkedIn stories aren't about big wins. They're about moments of growth.

Priya's post about the client meeting wasn't about a victory. It was about what the mistake taught her.

That's what makes employee stories powerful: they're real. Vulnerable. Growth-oriented.

You don't need to announce achievements to have a story worth telling. You need to share what changed your thinking.

Story Structure: The Four-Step Formula

Here's a structure you can use for almost any LinkedIn story:

Step 1: Start with the Scene

Describe where you were or what happened. Be specific enough to create a visual.

Weak opening:

"I recently had a meeting that taught me about listening."

Strong opening:

"Last Tuesday, I walked into a client presentation at their Lower Parel office, confident I'd solved their problem. I'd spent three weeks researching, building models, perfecting the solution. When I finished, the client leaned back and said: 'This is impressive work. But it doesn't solve our actual problem.'"

The strong version puts you there. You can feel the confidence turning to confusion, the three weeks of work suddenly questioned.

Step 2: Add the Emotion

Share what you felt or noticed in that moment. This is what makes stories human.

Example:

"I felt my stomach drop. I'd been so focused on building something impressive that I'd stopped listening to what they actually needed. The drive back to my office through Mumbai traffic felt endless—ninety minutes of replaying our conversations, realizing all the signals I'd missed."

This creates empathy. Your audience has been there. They remember that feeling.

Step 3: Reveal the Insight

Explain what changed. What you realized. What you learned. What you did differently afterward.

Example:

"That moment taught me something I wish I'd learned earlier: Expertise means nothing if you're solving the wrong problem. Now, before building anything, I spend twice as long listening, asking questions, and confirming understanding. I'd rather look less impressive early and deliver something useful than showcase brilliance that misses the mark."

This is the professional value. The audience walks away with a lesson they can apply.

Step 4: End with Reflection or Invitation

Close with a thought that invites others into conversation.

Example:

"When have you realized you were solving the wrong problem because you stopped listening?"

This transforms your post from monologue to dialogue. People engage because you've invited them to share their experience.

The Complete Formula:

$$\text{Scene} \rightarrow \text{Emotion} \rightarrow \text{Insight} \rightarrow \text{Reflection}$$

Simple. Repeatable. Powerful.

Priya's process:

"After that first post, I started looking for stories everywhere," she said. "Not big dramatic moments—just moments where I learned something. A comment from a junior colleague. A client question I couldn't answer. A process that failed. Once you start looking, you realize."

Three Types of Stories That Work for Employees

Story Type 1: The Small Moment

Not every story needs high stakes. Sometimes the best insights come from quiet observations.

Example:

"I was mentoring a junior colleague yesterday who asked me a question I couldn't answer. My first instinct was to make something up—to maintain the illusion that seniority means knowing everything. Instead, I said: 'I don't know.

Let's figure it out together.' That moment reminded me: Curiosity keeps us humble, no matter how long we've been in the job. What's a question you couldn't answer that made you better at what you do?"

Why it works:

- ✓ Relatable moment (everyone mentors or is mentored)
- ✓ Vulnerable admission (resisting the urge to fake expertise)
- ✓ Universal lesson (humility, curiosity)
- ✓ Invitation to engage (question at the end)

Story Type 2: The Team Moment

These stories show culture in action. They humanize your organization and reveal your values.

Example:

"Last month, our team missed a major deadline. We were all bracing for the post-mortem meeting, expecting blame and pressure. Instead, our manager opened with one question: 'What did we learn, and what do we need to change?' That single question shifted the entire conversation—from defense to reflection, from blame to strategy. I've been in a lot of meetings since then, but I keep coming back to that question. It's what separates teams that improve from teams that just survive."

Why it works:

- ✓ Specific situation (missed deadline, expected blame)
- ✓ Surprising turn (manager's question shifts tone)
- ✓ Lesson extracted (blame versus learning)
- ✓ Transferable insight (readers can use that question)

Story Type 3: The Purpose Moment

These stories connect daily work to larger meaning. They remind people why what you do matters.

Example:

"During a client call last week, someone thanked us for 'making their process simpler.' It was a passing comment, barely two seconds long. But it stopped me in my tracks. We'd spent six months building this tool. Late nights. Frustrating bugs. Endless revisions. And all of it came down to this: someone's job got easier. Not revolutionary. Not headline-making. Just easier. That reminder mattered: Real impact often comes from invisible work, from the details no one notices until they work the way they should. What's a 'small' project that taught you something big?"

Why it works:

- ✓ Emotional moment (gratitude for work often unseen)
- ✓ Behind-the-scenes reality (late nights, bugs, effort)
- ✓ Reframe (small work = big impact)
- ✓ Universal truth (invisible work matters)

Avoiding the Storytelling Pitfalls

Storytelling can go wrong when it loses balance. Here's what to watch for:

Pitfall 1: Too Self-Focused

If the story becomes about showing off, it loses authenticity.

Red flag: "Here's how I single-handedly saved the project . . ."

Better: "Here's what our team learned when the project almost failed . . ."

Focus on the lesson, not the achievement. People remember insights, not accomplishments.

Pitfall 2: Too Vague

A story without a clear point leaves readers wondering why they read it.

Red flag: "Had an interesting day at work. Lots to think about."

Better: Include specific scene, specific emotion, specific insight.

Pitfall 3: Too Emotional Without Context

Vulnerability is powerful, but it must serve a purpose. Share what you learned, not just how you felt.

Red flag: "Today was really hard. I'm struggling."

Better: "Today was really hard. Here's what it taught me about resilience . . ."

Pitfall 4: Too Corporate

Avoid sounding like a press release. LinkedIn readers respond to warmth, not slogans.

Red flag: "Proud to work for an organization that values innovation, collaboration, and excellence."

Better: "Yesterday our team tried something new. It failed. But our manager's response—'What did we learn?'—showed me what collaboration actually looks like."

Remember: Authenticity isn't oversharing. It's being real with intention.

Priya's guideline:

"I ask myself: Would I tell this story to a colleague over chai? If yes, I post it. If it feels too personal or too performative, I don't. The test is simple: Does this help someone else, or does it just make me look good?"

The Power of Repetition (Why Storytelling Is a Practice)

The more you tell stories, the easier it becomes.

Over time, you'll notice patterns—recurring themes that reflect who you are and what you value. Those themes often become your content pillars.

Priya discovered this after six months of posting.

She noticed that her most engaging posts shared a pattern: they were all about moments when technical excellence missed the human element. That became one of her content pillars: "Listening Before Building."

Once she recognized the pattern, finding stories became easier. She knew what to look for in her daily work.

Storytelling isn't a one-time skill. It's a habit.

Every week, ask yourself:

✓ What moment stayed with me?

✓ What did I learn this week that might help someone else?

✓ What surprised me, challenged me, or changed my thinking?

That's your next story.

In 2008, psychologist K. Anders Ericsson published research on what he called "deliberate practice." He found that experts don't become experts simply by doing something repeatedly. They become experts by doing it with intention—seeking feedback, noticing what works, and refining their approach.

The same applies to storytelling.

The more you practice, the more you notice which stories resonate. You begin to see patterns. You refine your instinct for what makes a moment worth sharing.

Priya's first 10 posts averaged 40 likes. Her next 20 posts averaged 120 reactions and 15 comments. Not because her stories got more dramatic—but because she got better at recognizing which moments had lessons worth extracting.

Practice with feedback is what turns posting into storytelling.

Priya's evolution:

"Six months after that first post, I looked back at my early attempts and cringed," she said with a laugh. "They were so generic. 'Grateful for this opportunity.' 'Proud of my team.' All true, but empty. Now I know: if I can't tell you the specific moment, the specific emotion, the specific lesson—I don't post it. Specificity is what makes stories real."

What Happened to Priya (One Year Later)

One year after that parking lot moment in Lower Parel, Priya had:

✓ **Spoken at three industry conferences** (Bangalore, Delhi, Mumbai)

✓ **Built a LinkedIn following of 4,200+** (from 680 before the post)

✓ **Received seven consulting inquiries** specifically mentioning her "client listening" expertise

✓ **Been invited to write a column** for an Indian business publication

✓ **Trained her company's junior consultants** on client engagement

But the most meaningful outcome wasn't professional.

Six months after her post, she received a message from a young consultant in Chennai:

"I read your post about the Lower Parel meeting. I had a similar moment last week—I'd built the wrong solution. Your post made me realize I wasn't alone. It gave me the courage to admit the mistake to my client, rebuild the right way, and actually strengthen the relationship. Thank you for being honest about your experience."

Priya still has that message saved.

"That's when I understood," she told me during our conversation at a café near her Andheri apartment. "Storytelling on LinkedIn isn't about building a personal brand or getting speaking gigs. Those are byproducts. The real value is in giving someone else permission to be human. To admit mistakes. To learn out loud. That parking lot moment was painful. But sharing it? That turned pain into purpose."

She paused, stirring her chai.

"I used to think LinkedIn was about showcasing success. Now I know: it's about sharing growth. And growth always starts with a moment where you realize you got it wrong."

That's the power of employee storytelling.

Not perfect stories. True ones.

Not polished narratives. Honest ones.

Not press releases. Moments of being human.

Your story is already there. You just have to tell it.

9 The Psychology of Attention: Writing for the Brain

Two Professionals, Same Strategy, Different Results

Maria Tan and Alex Wang both work in Singapore's financial district.

They've never met. They work for different companies—Maria at a global investment bank in Raffles Place, and Alex at a fintech startup in one of the gleaming towers near Marina Bay.

But for six months in 2023, they followed remarkably similar LinkedIn strategies:

Both posted twice a week (Tuesday and Thursday mornings)

Both wrote about fintech and digital banking

Both had 10+ years of industry experience

Both crafted thoughtful, well-researched content

After six months, here were their results:

MARIA'S AVERAGE POST:

- Twenty-two reactions (mostly from colleagues)
- Two to three comments (polite, generic)
- Forty-five profile views per week

- Zero speaking invitations

- Zero job offers

- Feeling: Frustrated, invisible, considering quitting LinkedIn

ALEX'S AVERAGE POST:

- 230 reactions (from across Southeast Asia and beyond)

- Thirty-five to forty comments (meaningful, from industry leaders)

- 180 profile views per week

- Three speaking invitations (including FinTech Festival Singapore)

- Two job offers (one from a US company, one from a regional bank)

- Feeling: Confident, connected, building real momentum

Same industry. Same city. Same experience level. Dramatically different outcomes.

What was the difference?

Maria wrote for the algorithm. Alex wrote for the brain.

Let me show you exactly what that means.

Maria's Approach: Professional but Forgettable

Here's a typical Maria post:

"5 Key Trends in Digital Banking for 2024

As we navigate the evolving landscape of financial technology, it's important to consider several emerging trends that will shape the industry:

1. AI-powered customer service solutions

2. Blockchain integration in cross-border payments

3. Enhanced cybersecurity measures

4. Open banking APIs

5. Sustainable finance initiatives

These developments represent significant opportunities for innovation and growth. Financial institutions should carefully evaluate how to incorporate these trends into their strategic planning.

What trends are you seeing in your organization? #FinTech #DigitalBanking #Innovation"

Analysis:

✓ **Professional**

✓ **Informative**

✓ **Well-organized**

✖ **Generic** (could have been written by anyone)

✖ **No emotional hook** (brain says "this can wait")

✖ **High cognitive load** (five topics = overwhelming)

✖ **Weak opening** (brain decides in first line: "I've seen this before")

✖ **Passive voice** ("should be evaluated" instead of "you should evaluate")

Result: Twenty-two likes from colleagues who felt obligated. Zero comments with substance. Post disappeared within three hours.

Maria's frustration:

"I spend 45 minutes researching and writing each post," she told a colleague over coffee at a Tanjong Pagar café. "I make sure everything is accurate and professional. But nobody engages. Am I just not interesting enough for LinkedIn?"

Alex's Approach: Brain-First Writing

Here's a typical Alex post from the same period:

"I thought I understood customer behavior. Then an 83-year-old woman taught me I knew nothing.

Last Tuesday, she walked into our bank's pilot branch in Chinatown. We'd just launched our 'digital-first' experience—sleek tablets, QR codes, minimal staff.

She looked around, confused. Tried to use the tablet. Failed. Tried again. Started to leave.

I stopped her. Asked if I could help.

She said: 'I just want to deposit $50. Why does everything need to be so complicated?'

That sentence changed how I think about innovation.

Here's what she taught me about the gap between what we build and what people actually need . . . [continued]

What obvious things have customers taught you that all the market research missed?"

Analysis:

- ✓ **Immediate tension** ("I thought I understood . . . then someone taught me I knew nothing")
- ✓ **Specific story** (eight-three-year-old woman in Chinatown branch)
- ✓ **Emotional hook** (confusion, failure, realization)
- ✓ **One clear idea** (digital innovation versus customer needs)
- ✓ **Visual** (you can picture the scene)
- ✓ **Vulnerable** (admits what he didn't know)
- ✓ **Invitation** (asks a question that others can answer)

Result: 287 reactions. Forty-two comments (including one from a senior VP at DBS Bank who invited Alex to speak at an internal summit). Post stayed in feed for 18+ hours, reached people across Southeast Asia.

Alex's reflection:

"I used to write like a consultant presenting findings," he told his manager during their one-on-one at their Marina Bay office. "Bullet points. Frameworks. Very professional. Very boring. When I started telling stories about real moments, everything changed."

The Difference: Understanding How Brains Actually Work

Maria and Alex weren't writing for different audiences. They were both targeting financial services professionals in Southeast Asia.

The difference was understanding one fundamental truth:

The brain doesn't evaluate content rationally. It decides emotionally, then justifies logically.

In the three seconds after someone sees your post, their brain isn't asking:

- "Is this person credible?"
- "Is this information accurate?"
- "Does this align with industry best practices?"

The brain is asking three primal questions:

1. **Is this relevant to me?**
   Maria's opening: "As we navigate the evolving landscape . . ."
   Brain response: *Vague. Generic. Scroll.*
   Alex's opening: "I thought I understood customer behavior. Then an 83-year-old woman taught me I knew nothing."
   Brain response: *Tension. Surprise. Story. Stay.*

2. **Is this emotionally engaging?**
   Maria's post: Lists trends with no human element
   Brain response: *Information I can Google. Scroll.*
   Alex's post: Human struggling, failing, learning

3. **Brain response:** *I've felt that confusion. I want to know what happened.*

4. **Is this different from what I just saw?**
   Maria's post: "5 Key Trends" (seen 100 times this week)
   Brain response: *Same as every other post. Scroll.*
   Alex's post: Specific story about specific person in specific place
   Brain response: *I've never heard this story. Stay.*

These aren't conscious decisions. They happen in three seconds, driven by brain chemistry older than civilization.

This chapter shows you how to write for those three seconds—and turn them into three minutes of engaged attention.

The Three-Second Decision

There's a moment that happens every time someone encounters your LinkedIn post.

It's not conscious. It happens faster than thought.

Their eyes land on the first line. Their brain makes a split-second calculation:

"Is this worth my time?"

If the answer is yes, they keep reading. If the answer is no—or even "maybe"—they scroll.

You have about three seconds to earn a "yes."

Not three minutes. Not thirty seconds. Three seconds.

In that window, the brain isn't evaluating logic, credentials, or the sophistication of your argument. It's asking those three primal questions we just saw with Maria and Alex:

1. Is this relevant to me?

2. Is this emotionally engaging?

3. Is this different from what I just saw?

These questions aren't new. They're the same neural circuits that drove our ancestors to notice movement in tall grass (relevance), react to a baby's cry (emotion), and investigate an unusual sound (novelty).

The algorithms have changed. Human attention hasn't.

This chapter isn't about gaming LinkedIn's algorithm. It's about understanding how the human brain decides what deserves attention—and how to write posts that respect that biology.

Because here's the truth: the algorithm decides who sees your content. But the brain decides whether they stay.

And reach follows retention.

The Attention Paradox

A joint study by Microsoft and the University of Toronto found that the average human attention span has dropped to just 8.25 seconds, down from 12 seconds in 2000.

That sounds catastrophic for anyone trying to communicate anything meaningful.

But here's what that statistic misses: the brain's ability to sustain deep attention hasn't disappeared. It's simply become more selective.

We'll scroll past a hundred posts in thirty seconds. Then we'll read a 2,000-word article that holds our attention for ten minutes straight.

The difference isn't our capacity for focus. It's whether the content earns that focus in the first three seconds.

LinkedIn's research confirms this pattern: posts that keep users reading longer (measured by dwell time) outperform others by up to 3× in organic reach.

The platform treats dwell time as a critical signal of value. In their 2024 algorithm update, LinkedIn confirmed: "Posts that make people stop, think, and stay are prioritized in the feed."

The data back this:

- Posts that evoke awe, curiosity, or surprise generate 2× higher dwell time than purely informational content
- Posts with story-based tension get 58% more comments than generic announcements (LinkedIn Engagement Report, 2024)
- Multi-slide carousels increase viewing duration by 3× compared to single-image posts (Social Insider, 2024)

Translation: If you can earn three seconds of attention, you can earn three minutes.

The question is: how do you earn those first three seconds?

The answer lies in understanding not how algorithms work, but how brains work.

Maria's posts earned polite scrolls. Alex's posts earned attention. Let's break down why.

The Neurochemistry of Curiosity (Why Open Loops Work)

In 2014, neuroscientist Matthias Gruber at UC Davis conducted an experiment that changed how we understand curiosity.

He put participants in an fMRI scanner and showed them trivia questions. Some questions sparked intense curiosity ("What famous rock band once got banned from playing at a hotel for tossing a TV out the window?"). Others generated mild interest. Others, none at all.

Then he tracked what happened in their brains when they felt curious about the answer.

What he discovered was remarkable:

Curiosity activates the brain's reward circuitry—specifically the caudate nucleus and hippocampus—releasing dopamine and improving information retention by up to 25%.

The brain treats curiosity like hunger. It craves resolution.

That's why open loops work so well on LinkedIn:

Weak opening (Maria's style):

"Here are three lessons about leadership I learned this quarter."

The brain knows exactly where this is going. No tension. No urgency. Scroll.

Strong opening (Alex's style):

"The biggest leadership mistake I made this quarter cost us a major client. Here's what I learned."

"Biggest mistake?" "Lost a client?" "What happened?" The brain leans in. Dopamine fires. You keep reading.

This isn't manipulation. It's honoring how attention works.

The brain doesn't want bland predictability. It wants surprises, tension, resolution—stories that move.

Give it what it wants.

Alex's discovery:

"I used to think opening with tension was clickbait," Alex told his team during a presentation at their startup's office overlooking Marina Bay. "But then I realized:

tension isn't manipulation. It's storytelling. Every good story has tension. Why should LinkedIn posts be different?"

Maria's learning curve:

Six months into her frustration, Maria attended a content writing workshop in Singapore. The instructor showed two LinkedIn posts side by side—one was Maria's (anonymized), one was similar to Alex's approach.

"Which one would you read?" the instructor asked.

Maria raised her hand for the second one. Then realized: *That's not how I write. That's the problem.*

Emotion Drives Memory (And Memory Drives Reach)

According to Harvard Business Review (2024), emotionally charged posts are 70% more likely to be remembered and reshared than neutral ones.

Emotion doesn't just capture attention. It makes that attention sticky.

This isn't new science. In 1977, psychologist Gordon Bower demonstrated what he called "mood-congruent memory." People remember information better when it's tied to emotion.

On LinkedIn, this means:

A post that makes someone feel something—understood, challenged, inspired, moved—will stick in their memory far longer than a post that simply informs.

Example of neutral (forgettable):

Maria's version:

"Our team completed the Q3 project ahead of schedule. Great work, everyone."

No emotion. No tension. No reason to remember.

Example of emotional (memorable):

Alex's version:

"Our team almost missed the Q3 deadline. Two weeks out, we realized our approach wouldn't work. We had to scrap three months of work and start over. The night we shipped it—on time—I watched our lead engineer cry in the conference room. Not from exhaustion. From pride. That's the kind of team I'm grateful to work with."

See the difference?

The second post makes you **feel** something. You remember the engineer crying. You remember pride, pressure, recovery. You remember the story.

And what you remember, you engage with. What you engage with, LinkedIn amplifies.

Emotion isn't optional for reach. It's required.

Maria's adjustment:

After the workshop, Maria rewrote her approach. Instead of "5 Key Trends in Digital Banking," she posted:

"A customer called me crying yesterday. Not angry—grateful. Our new digital loan approval process helped her get funding for her hawker stall in 24 hours. The old system would have taken 3 weeks. She said: 'You saved my business.' That's why I work in fintech."

Result: 156 reactions, 28 comments, 3 shares—7× her previous average.

Maria's realization:

"I was so focused on sounding professional that I forgot people connect with people, not bullet points."

Cognitive Load Theory (Why Less Is More)

In 1956, psychologist George Miller published one of the most influential papers in cognitive science: "The Magical Number Seven, Plus or Minus Two."

He argued that humans can hold about seven items in working memory at a time. But more recent research by **Nelson Cowan** (2010) suggests the actual number is closer to four items.

What this means for LinkedIn:

Your brain can only process a limited amount of information at once. When posts try to cover five topics, include ten insights, and reference three frameworks, the brain gets overwhelmed.

Overwhelm = scroll.

Clarity = stay.

The principle: One post, one idea.

Weak post (too much cognitive load)—Maria's old style:

"Five leadership lessons I learned this quarter: delegation, communication, strategic thinking, emotional intelligence, and time management. Here's how each applies . . ."

The brain sees five distinct topics and thinks: "This will take work." Scroll.

Strong post (manageable cognitive load)—Alex's style:

"The leadership lesson that surprised me most this quarter: Sometimes the best thing you can say in a meeting is nothing at all. Here's when silence became my strongest tool . . ."

One idea. One story. One takeaway. The brain thinks: "I can process this." Stay.

Concise posts with one clear idea outperform dense multi-topic ones.

Not because people are lazy. Because clarity is kindness to the reader's brain.

What Maria changed:

> **Before:** "5 Key Trends in Digital Banking"
>
> **After:** "The one customer insight that changed how I think about mobile banking"
>
> **Before:** 22 reactions
>
> **After:** 134 reactions

One idea. Deeper exploration. Better retention.

The Biases That Shape Engagement

Our brains rely on mental shortcuts—cognitive biases—that subtly influence why we stop, click, or scroll.

Understanding these biases is your competitive advantage.

BIAS 1: The Mere-Exposure Effect (Familiarity Builds Trust)

In the 1960s, psychologist Robert Zajonc showed Chinese characters to English-speaking participants. Some characters appeared once. Others appeared multiple times.

When asked which characters they preferred, participants overwhelmingly chose the ones they'd seen more often—even though they had no idea what any of them meant.

Zajonc called this the **"mere-exposure effect."** Repeated exposure increases liking, even for neutral stimuli.

Application for LinkedIn:

Consistency breeds trust. The more your audience sees your name and voice, the more comfortable they become engaging with you.

This is why posting weekly for a year beats posting daily for a month. The algorithm rewards consistency, yes—but more importantly, the human brain rewards familiarity.

Alex's consistency: Twice a week, every week, for eighteen months

Maria's inconsistency: Posted sporadically, sometimes 3× a week, then nothing for two weeks

BIAS 2: Social Proof (We Trust What Others Trust)

Humans look to others to decide what matters.

One study published in ScienceDirect (2023) found that visible engagement cues increased perceived credibility by 32%—even when the content itself was identical.

People didn't evaluate the information differently. They simply trusted it more because others had validated it first.

Application for LinkedIn:

Encourage interaction early:

- Ask a question in your post

- Tag relevant collaborators (meaningfully, not spammy)

- Reply to the first few comments quickly

Early engagement signals value. That signal attracts more engagement. The flywheel spins.

Alex's practice: Responds to first five comments within ten minutes

Maria's practice: Checks LinkedIn once a day, responds hours later

BIAS 3: Reciprocity (Give First, Receive Second)

In his landmark book *Influence*, Robert Cialdini describes reciprocity as one of the most powerful psychological triggers. We feel obligated to return favors, even small ones.

Application for LinkedIn:

Comment thoughtfully on others' posts before expecting engagement on yours.

LinkedIn's internal data shows that people who comment on peers' content receive 4.6× more engagement on their own posts.

This isn't manipulation. It's community building. You give attention before asking for it.

Alex's ritual: Spends fifteen minutes every morning commenting on three to five posts before posting his own

Maria's old habit: Posted, then hoped for engagement

BIAS 4: The Negativity Bias (Problems Grab Attention)

Our brains evolved to prioritize threats. Negative information captures attention faster and holds it longer than positive information.

Application for LinkedIn:

Start with tension, not perfection.

Weak opening: "We succeeded again this quarter!"

Strong opening: "We almost failed this quarter. Here's what saved us."

The second creates immediate tension. The brain wants resolution. You keep reading.

Important caveat: Don't manufacture drama. Share real challenges and real lessons. Authenticity matters more than engagement.

Why Stories with Tension Outperform "Feel-Good" Posts

The brain loves contrast: struggle before success, tension before resolution.

In 2010, neuroscientist Uri Hasson at Princeton conducted a fascinating experiment.

He had someone tell a story while lying in an fMRI scanner. Then he had listeners hear the same story, also while being scanned.

What he found was extraordinary:

When a story follows a narrative arc—conflict, climax, resolution—the listener's brain syncs with the storyteller's. Brain activity literally mirrors itself across both people.

Hasson called this phenomenon "neural coupling."

This synchronization increases empathy and comprehension. It's why a vulnerable story like "We lost a major client. Here's what I learned" will outperform "Grateful for my amazing team!" every single time.

LinkedIn's own analytics reflect this pattern:

- Posts that share a clear challenge and learning moment achieve 61% more saves (the strongest indicator of deep resonance)

- Posts written as first-person reflections with emotional tension hold users' attention 2.5× longer than neutral updates (LinkedIn Thought Leadership Index, 2024)

The formula:

Generic feel-good post (Maria's old style):

"Proud of my team for shipping this quarter's project!"

Story with tension (Alex's approach):

"Two weeks before deadline, our lead developer quit. The rest of the team looked at me like I had the answer. I didn't. But here's what we figured out together . . ."

The first might get some polite likes from colleagues.

The second creates neural coupling. People feel the panic, the uncertainty, the resolution. They experience the story, not just read it.

So if you want to stop the scroll: don't tell a perfect story. Tell a true one.

The Science of "Stopping Power" (Why the First Three Lines Matter)

Eye-tracking studies by Nielsen Norman Group show that people read only 20% of the text on an average webpage. But they spend 57% of their time on the first screenful.

Translation: The first three lines of your post determine its life or death.

On LinkedIn, those three lines appear before someone clicks "See more." They're your billboard. Your hook. Your only chance to earn attention.

Weak first three lines (Maria's old approach):

"I've been thinking a lot about leadership lately. There are so many different approaches, and I wanted to share some thoughts about what's been working for me. Here are three lessons . . ."

The brain reads this and thinks: "Vague. Slow. I'll scroll."

Strong first three lines (Alex's approach):

"I fired someone yesterday. It was the right decision and the hardest conversation I've had in years. Here's what I learned about when compassion looks like letting someone go."

The brain reads this and thinks: "Tension. Vulnerability. Specific. I need to know what happens."

The tactics that create stopping power:

1. **Start with a short, high-contrast sentence (under twelve words)**
   "The best idea I had this year started as a mistake."
   "We lost $400,000 in three weeks."
   "My boss called me into her office at 4 pm on Friday."

2. **Use strong first verbs**

   Not "I've been thinking . . ."

   But "I realized . . ." or "We failed . . ." or "Here's what surprised me . . ."

   Strong verbs signal movement, not meandering."

3. **Create immediate tension or curiosity**

   "The biggest leadership mistake I made . . ."

   "Nobody told me this about [X], so I'm telling you . . ."

   "Five years ago, I would have made a completely different decision."

4. **Add white space**

   Don't write a paragraph as the opening. Write one to two sentences,
   then break.

   Visual breathing room signals readability. The brain thinks: "This won't be exhausting. I'll keep reading."

   The test:

   Look at your last five posts. Read only the first three lines.

   Would you keep reading? If not, neither will your audience.

   Rewrite those openings. Watch your engagement transform.

   How to Write for the Brain, Not the Algorithm

   Here's your practical framework:

   1. HOOK WITH NOVELTY

   Begin with curiosity, conflict, or a surprising fact.

   Example: "The best idea I had this year started as a mistake."

   This activates the brain's prediction error system. It wants to resolve the gap between expectation and reality.

   2. FOLLOW THE ARC

   Structure your post like a story: **Tension → Insight → Resolution.**

   Not: "Here are three lessons about [topic]."

   But: "I thought I understood [topic]. Then this happened. Here's what changed my mind."

3. ONE IDEA PER POST

Respect cognitive load. One clear idea is memorable. Five ideas in one post create overwhelm.

4. USE SHORT PARAGRAPHS

Two to three lines maximum. White space signals accessibility.

5. BUILD SOCIAL TRIGGERS

Tag others meaningfully (not spammy). Reply to comments quickly. Use reciprocity.

6. DESIGN FOR DWELL TIME

Use carousels or "See more" breaks strategically to increase time on post. LinkedIn's 2024 algorithm update confirms: **longer dwell time = wider distribution.**

7. END WITH INVITATION, NOT DECLARATION

Don't just make a point. Invite response.

Weak ending: "That's my take on leadership."

Strong ending: "That's what worked for me. What's your experience?"

Questions, invitations, and open loops drive comments. Comments drive reach.

What Happened Next: Maria and Alex, Twelve Months Later

Maria's transformation:

After the workshop, Maria changed her entire approach. She spent one week analyzing Alex's posts (they still didn't know each other) and other high-engagement content from Singapore's fintech scene.

Her new strategy:

- One idea per post (no more "5 trends" lists)

- Start with a story, not a framework

- Show vulnerability, not just expertise

- Respond to comments within the first hour

- Comment on five others' posts before posting her own

Maria's results after six months:

- Average reactions: 22 → 167 (7.5× increase)

- Average comments: 2 → 24 (12× increase)

- Profile views: 45/week → 210/week (4.6× increase)

- Speaking invitations: 0 → 2 (including panel at Singapore FinTech Festival)

- Job inquiries: 0 → 4 (including one from a US fintech)

Maria's reflection:

"I thought being professional meant being formal. I was wrong. Being professional means being clear, honest, and helpful. The brain doesn't care about bullet points. It cares about people."

Alex's continued growth:

Alex kept refining his approach, running small experiments:

- Testing different opening lines

- Tracking which stories got most saves

- Noting which questions drove best discussions

Alex's results after eighteen months:

- Average reactions: 230 → 380

- Average comments: 35 → 58

- Speaking invitations: 3 → 7

- Consulting offers: 0 → 2

- Book deal: 1 (writing about fintech innovation in Southeast Asia)

Alex's advice:

"Everyone thinks they need to be clever or have perfect insights. You don't. You need to be human. The brain recognizes human instantly. Everything else is just noise."

They finally met:

In December 2024, at the Singapore FinTech Festival, Maria was speaking on a panel about digital banking innovation. In the audience: Alex.

After the panel, he introduced himself. They compared notes over coffee at a Marina Bay café.

"I've been following your posts," Alex said. "You've really found your voice."

Maria laughed. "I've been following yours too. You're the reason I changed my approach."

They've been LinkedIn connections ever since. They comment on each other's posts. They've collaborated on two articles. They both speak at the same conference circuit.

Same industry. Same city. Same platform.

Different approach. Different results.

The difference? Understanding how brains work.

Practical Exercises (Do These This Week)

Exercise 1: Hook Audit (fifteen minutes)

Review your last five posts. Did you start with tension, surprise, or curiosity?

If not, rewrite one. Compare the engagement.

Exercise 2: Story Loop Practice (twenty minutes)

Take a recent work experience. Write it twice:

Version A: Straightforward summary

Version B: Story with tension (problem → struggle → resolution)

Notice how differently they feel.

Exercise 3: First-Three-Lines Test (ten minutes)

Look at your next draft post. Read only the first three lines.

Ask: **"Would I keep reading?"**

If no, rewrite until yes.

Exercise 4: Reciprocity Ritual (fifteen minutes Before Posting)

Spend fifteen minutes engaging on others' content before you post your own.

Leave three to five thoughtful comments. Tag someone whose work you appreciate.

Then publish your post. Watch your visibility improve.

IV Technical Excellence— Format, Features, and Optimization

You know what to say and how to tell your story. Now let's master the mechanics that amplify reach. This section covers the technical details that separate posts that get buried from posts that break through: optimal formats, strategic timing, the features that extend your influence, and the settings that protect your brand. Good content deserves good execution.

10 Technical Best Practices: Photos, Videos, Timing, and Algorithm

The Same Post, Different Results

In January 2024, Miguel Santos posted the same content twice on LinkedIn.

Miguel had been a product manager at a mid-sized tech company in Metro Manila for five years—quietly building features and frameworks while watching colleagues with less experience gain more visibility on LinkedIn.

His work was solid. His insights were valuable. The features he'd shipped served hundreds of thousands of users across Southeast Asia.

But his LinkedIn presence? Nearly invisible.

"I'd spend two hours stuck in Manila traffic scrolling through LinkedIn," he told me over video call last month. "Watching people post about the same problems I'd already solved. Getting thousands of reactions while my posts got . . . maybe eight likes from the same people every time."

He'd started to internalize it. *Maybe I'm just not interesting enough. Maybe what works here doesn't matter globally. Maybe nobody cares about product work happening in the Philippines.*

One Sunday evening, after another week of being overlooked in team discussions while less experienced colleagues' LinkedIn posts were getting referenced in meetings, Miguel decided to share a framework he'd developed for prioritizing product features.

This wasn't theory. It had actually saved his team four months of wasted effort and helped them ship a feature that increased user retention by 23%.

He posted it twice, one week apart, using the exact same content.

Post A (Monday morning):

- Plain text explanation

- External link to his blog in the main post

- Posted at 6:30 AM Manila time (before his first coffee, rushing to get it out before his commute)

- No hashtags

- No visual element

Results: 740 impressions, 8 likes, and 0 comments

Miguel stared at his phone on the jeepney ride to work. *See? Nobody cares what I have to say.*

He texted his colleague Maya: "Tried posting that framework. Eight likes. Same people as always. I give up."

Maya called him immediately.

"Miguel, you're one of the smartest product people I know. The problem isn't your content. The problem is you posted a text blob with a blog link at 6:30 in the morning. Let me help you try one more time."

She convinced him to post again—with a few technical changes.

Post B (Wednesday morning, one week later):

- Same content reformatted as a five-slide carousel

- No external links (just the carousel itself)

- Posted at 8:15 AM Manila time

- Three relevant hashtags
- He replied to the first three comments within twenty minutes

Results: 28,470 impressions, 350 reactions, 53 comments, and 12 saves

Miguel was in a meeting when his phone started buzzing. He glanced down and saw notification after notification rolling in.

By lunch, his post had reached product managers in Singapore, Australia, India, and even a few in the United States. Someone from Grab commented. Someone from Shopee shared it. A product leader in Jakarta sent him a DM asking if they could feature his framework in their team workshop.

"I literally just sat in the pantry staring at my phone," Miguel said. "Same framework. Same insights. Same network."

38× more reach.

What changed?

Not the quality of his thinking. Not the value of his framework. Not his expertise or credibility.

What changed was the technical execution.

The mechanics of posting on LinkedIn matter more than most people realize. The right format, timing, and technical choices can mean the difference between feeling invisible and finally being heard.

This chapter breaks down the tactical decisions that amplified Miguel's content—not through tricks or hacks, but through understanding how the platform's systems actually work.

Because great content with poor execution is invisible.

And good content with smart execution is unavoidable.

The Algorithm Shift: What Actually Matters Now

For years, LinkedIn's algorithm was simple: likes = reach.

The more likes a post got, the more people saw it. So everyone optimized for likes—posting inspirational quotes, feel-good stories, anything that generated quick double-taps.

Then LinkedIn changed the game.

In their 2024 algorithm update, the platform made a crucial shift: not all engagement signals are created equal.

The new hierarchy of engagement signals:

TIER 1 (Highest Value): Saves & Shares

When someone saves your post (bookmarks it for later) or reposts/shares it, that tells the algorithm: *"This content is valuable enough to keep or amplify."*

TIER 2 (High Value): Comments

Especially meaningful comments (3+ words that add perspective), not just emoji reactions.

TIER 3 (Medium Value): Reactions

Likes, loves, celebrates—these still matter, but carry less weight than they used to.

Why the shift?

A like is often impulsive—a quick tap while scrolling.

But a save says: *"This content is worth coming back to."*

A share says: *"This content is worth sharing with my network."*

A comment says: *"This content sparked enough thought that I want to add to the conversation."*

These signals indicate deeper engagement, which is what LinkedIn wants to promote.

For employees building thought leadership, this changes everything.

Instead of chasing viral moments that generate thousands of likes, focus on creating posts that earn:

✓ **Saves** (frameworks, templates, guides, insights worth referencing)

✓ **Shares** (perspectives others want to amplify to their networks)

✓ **Comments** (questions, stories that invite dialogue)

Miguel's revelation:

Post A: 8 likes, 0 saves, and 0 comments

Post B: 187 reactions, **12 saves**, and **23 comments**

The algorithm noticed the saves and comments—and rewarded Post B with **38× more reach**.

"The moment I understood this, everything changed," Miguel said. "I stopped asking 'Will people like this?' and started asking 'Will people save this? Will they want to reference this later?'"

That shift in thinking transformed his content strategy.

Visual Formats: What Works (And Why)

Always include a visual when possible.

Posts with images, graphics, or documents significantly improve dwell time and visibility. But not all visual formats perform equally.

Format 1: Photos and Graphics

✓ Use high-quality, relevant images

✓ Native uploads (directly to LinkedIn) perform better than external links

✓ Design for mobile (60%+ of users browse on phones)

✓ Ensure text in images is readable on small screens

Performance: Solid baseline. Photos improve engagement by ~30% compared to text-only posts.

Format 2: Videos

✓ Keep it short (one to two minutes ideal, thirty to sixty seconds better)

✓ Open with strong visual hook (not logo or title slide)

✓ Include captions (70% of users watch on mute)

✓ Native upload (directly to LinkedIn, not YouTube link)

Performance: Can be high-impact, but harder to execute well. Video requires more production effort and competes with scrolling behavior.

Format 3: Carousels (The High-Performance Format)

This is where Miguel's **38× improvement** came from.

Carousels have emerged as LinkedIn's algorithmically favored format. Here's why:

1. **Dwell time:** Users spend more time swiping through slides, which signals quality content to LinkedIn

2. **Native content:** Carousels are uploaded directly to LinkedIn (not external links), which the algorithm prefers

3. **Engagement multiplier:** According to SocialPilot (2025), multi-image carousels average **6.60% engagement rate**—nearly double most other formats

4. **Second-degree reach:** Because carousels hold attention longer, they're more likely to be shown to your connections' connections

When to use carousels:

✓ Step-by-step explanations (*"How we solved this problem in 4 steps"*)

✓ Multi-layered insights (*"5 lessons from this project"*)

✓ Frameworks or models (*"The 3-part decision framework I use"*)

✓ Before/after stories (*"What changed after we did X"*)

Miguel's breakthrough:

His product prioritization framework was perfect for carousel format. Each slide built on the last, creating a complete mental model readers could save and reference.

"Maya sat with me at a coffee shop in BGC and we redesigned the whole thing as slides," Miguel said. "Five slides. One idea per slide. Big text. Simple visuals. Took us 90 minutes to create in Canva."

That ninety-minute investment generated 2,847 impressions.

Carousel Best Practices:

Slide 1 is everything: Your first slide is the billboard. Make it visually strong and clearly state what the audience will get:

- "3 Things I Learned Managing Remote Teams Across 4 Timezones"

- "How We Cut Meeting Time by 40% in 4 Steps"

- "The Framework That Saved Us 4 Months of Wasted Work"

Without a strong first slide, users won't swipe. Game over.

Keep it digestible: Three to ten slides is the sweet spot. Avoid twenty slides unless each adds clear, distinct value.

One idea per slide: Don't cram. Each slide should make one point clearly.

Design for mobile: Large text, high contrast, simple layouts. If it's not readable on a phone, it won't work.

End with invitation: Your final slide should ask a question or invite comment—this drives engagement that amplifies reach.

Track beyond likes: Monitor impressions, comments, shares, and especially dwell time (how many people scrolled through all slides).

Miguel's metrics:

His carousel had an **82% completion rate**—meaning 82% of people who started it, finished it.

That high dwell time is what triggered the algorithm to show it to thousands more people.

"When I saw that 82% completion rate, I understood," Miguel said. "People weren't just glancing at it. They were reading through the whole thing. That's what the algorithm rewards."

Links: The Platform Penalty

Here's something most people don't realize: LinkedIn's algorithm penalizes posts with external links in the main body.

Why? Because LinkedIn wants to keep users on LinkedIn. Every external link is a potential exit from the platform.

Miguel's Post A included a link to his blog. The algorithm saw this and thought: *"This post is trying to drive traffic away from LinkedIn. Suppress it."*

Miguel's Post B had no external links. The algorithm rewarded it with wider distribution.

"I was so proud of that blog post," Miguel said. "I spent hours writing it, formatting it, making it look professional. And by linking to it, I basically told LinkedIn: 'Hey, take people off your platform'. Of course it got suppressed."

The workaround:

If you need to include a link (to your blog, company page, external article):

Option 1: Put the link in the first comment

Publish your post without links, then immediately comment with: *"Full framework here: [link]"*

This keeps the main post "native" while still providing the resource.

Option 2: Provide summary + mention link in comments

Write the full insight in your post. Add at the end: *"Link to the full template in comments."*

Option 3: Use LinkedIn-native links when possible

Links to LinkedIn newsletters, LinkedIn articles, or other LinkedIn content aren't penalized the same way external links are.

The rule: If you want maximum reach, keep external links out of the main post body.

Miguel's current practice:

"Now I write everything natively on LinkedIn. If I want to include a link, I mention it in the post and drop it in the first comment. My reach has been consistently 20–30× higher than when I was linking out."

Timing: When the Algorithm Is Watching

The Critical First Hour

The first sixty minutes after you publish are make-or-break.

Here's how it works:

1. **You publish a post**

2. **LinkedIn shows it to a small sample of your network** (usually 5–10% of your followers)

3. **The algorithm watches:** How quickly do people engage? How meaningful is the engagement?

4. **Based on that initial signal, LinkedIn decides whether to amplify your post to a wider audience**

   If your post gets strong engagement in the first hour: LinkedIn shows it to more people, then watches again, then amplifies further. The flywheel spins.

   If your post gets weak engagement in the first hour: LinkedIn assumes it's not valuable and stops showing it. The post dies.

Miguel's timing mistake:

Post A: Posted at 6:30 AM Manila time, got two likes in the first hour (both from close colleagues). The algorithm marked it as low-value.

Post B: Posted at 8:15 AM Manila time, got fourteen reactions and three comments in the first hour. The algorithm amplified it.

"6:30 AM was too early," Miguel explained. "Most of my network in the Philippines hadn't started work yet. Singapore was just waking up. Australia was already mid-morning but not checking LinkedIn yet. The US and Europe were asleep. I posted into a void."

How to optimize for the first hour:

1. **Post when your audience is active**
   For most professional audiences, peak engagement times are:
   ✓ **Tuesday–Wednesday, 8–10 AM** (local time)
   ✓ **Early afternoons (1–2 PM)** work for some audiences

Miguel's timezone strategy (Philippines, GMT + 8):
• **8:15 AM Manila time** catches:

   ◆ Philippines professionals starting their workday

   ◆ Singapore/Malaysia at desks with morning coffee

- Australia mid-morning (checking LinkedIn between meetings)
- India just finishing lunch
- US West Coast evening (some checking before bed)

"8:15 AM turned out to be the sweet spot," Miguel said. "It's when the most people across Asia-Pacific are active, plus I catch some US folks wrapping up their day."

Check your analytics to see when YOUR audience is most active. Don't rely on general best practices.

2. **Engage actively in the first hour**

   Don't just post and walk away. The first hour requires:

   ✓ **Responding to early comments quickly** (this signals to the algorithm that conversation is happening)
   ✓ **Leaving a thoughtful first comment yourself** (this can jumpstart dialogue)
   ✓ **Tagging one to two relevant people** who might engage (meaningful tags, not spam)

Miguel's first-hour strategy:

"I set a 20-minute timer after posting. I replied to the first 3 comments within 12 minutes. That early activity told the algorithm: 'This post is generating conversation.'"

He also started leaving a first comment on his own posts:

"What's been your experience with product prioritization? Have you found frameworks helpful, or do you prefer a different approach?"

This gave people something to respond to even before others had commented.

3. **Don't post multiple times in twelve hours**

   If you post twice in quick succession, the algorithm may suppress both posts (spam detection) or split your audience's attention.

   Stick to one post per week maximum for most professionals. Quality over frequency.

Miguel's current rhythm:

Posts every Wednesday at 8:15 AM Manila time. Never more than once a week.

"I used to think I needed to post every day to stay visible," he said. "But one well-executed post per week gets me more reach than daily random thoughts ever did."

Hashtags and Tags: Strategic, Not Spammy

Hashtags:

Use **three to five relevant hashtags per post**. No more, no less.

Too few (zero to two): You miss categorization opportunities

Too many (more than six): You look spammy, algorithm penalizes

Choose narrow, relevant hashtags:

✖ #Success #Motivation #Leadership (too generic, millions of posts)

✓ #ProductManagement #ProductStrategy #B2BSaaS (specific, targeted)

Miguel's hashtags for Post B:

#ProductManagement #ProductPrioritization #ProductStrategy

"These hashtags helped my post surface to people interested in product topics—even beyond my immediate network," Miguel said. "I got engagement from product managers in Indonesia, Thailand, Vietnam who I'd never connected with."

Mentions (Tags):

Tag people **only when it adds genuine context:**

✓ You worked with them on the project

✓ You're quoting or referencing their work

✓ You think they'd add valuable perspective

✖ Mass-tagging unrelated people triggers spam filters

✖ Tagging senior leaders just to get their attention looks desperate

Miguel's approach:

He tagged Maya, the colleague who'd helped him develop the framework. She engaged immediately, which signaled credibility to the algorithm.

"Maya's comment in the first 10 minutes was huge," Miguel said. "She added her perspective, which made it a conversation, not just me broadcasting. The algorithm loves that."

The rule: Tags should feel natural, not performative.

Post Length and Structure: Optimizing for Readability

Ideal length: 170–400 words (~1,200–1,600 characters)

This is long enough to provide substance but short enough to maintain attention.

Structure for scannability:

1. **Strong hook (first one to two lines)**
   These lines appear before "See more." They determine whether people expand your post.
   ✘ "I've been thinking about leadership lately . . ."
   ✓ "We lost our best engineer last month. Here's what I learned about retention."

   Miguel's Post B hook:
   "We almost wasted 4 months building the wrong feature. This framework saved us."
   Short. Specific. Stakes clear.

2. **Short paragraphs (two to three lines maximum)**
   Long blocks of text create visual overwhelm. Break it up.

3. **White space**
   Give readers breathing room. Use line breaks generously.

4. **One clear idea**
   Don't try to cover five topics. One insight, well-developed, beats five insights rushed.

5. End with invitation

Close with a question or prompt that invites comments:

- "What's worked for you when prioritizing product features?"
- "Have you experienced this in your team?"
- "What would you add to this framework?"

Questions drive comments. Comments drive reach.

Miguel's ending:

"What's your approach to feature prioritization? Do you use frameworks, or have you found something else that works better?"

Twenty-three people responded with their own approaches, creating a thread that boosted the post's reach even further.

The Pre-Publish Checklist

Before you hit "Post," verify these elements:

- ☐ **Visual included** (photo, graphic, carousel, or video)
- ☐ **No external links in main post** (or link placed in comments)
- ☐ **One to two relevant tags** (people who genuinely add context)
- ☐ **Three to five specific hashtags** (narrow and relevant)
- ☐ **Posting at optimal time** (when your audience is active)
- ☐ **Strong hook in first one to two lines** (creates curiosity or tension)
- ☐ **One clear idea** (not five half-developed thoughts)
- ☐ **Invitation to comment** (question or prompt at the end)
- ☐ **Plan to engage in first hour** (twenty to thirty minutes set aside)

Miguel's Post A: Missed seven of these nine elements

Miguel's Post B: Hit all nine

The difference: 38× more reach

"I printed this checklist and stuck it on my monitor," Miguel said. "Now I go through it before every post. It's become automatic."

11 LinkedIn Features and Tools: Amplify Your Reach

The Discovery That Changed Her Strategy

For eight months, Sophie Dubois posted consistently on LinkedIn—twice a week, every week, sharing insights about HR strategy and workplace culture.

Sophie worked as an HR Strategy Lead at a mid-sized French tech scale-up in Paris. She'd been in HR for seven years, helping companies navigate the complex intersection of European labor laws, French workplace culture, and the always-on expectations of global tech.

Her posts were good. Thoughtful. Well-written—though she spent twice as long crafting them in English, her second language, always worried she'd make a grammatical mistake that would make her look unprofessional.

They averaged 150 reactions and a handful of comments.

But something bothered her: she was always starting from zero.

Every post reached roughly the same audience—her immediate network. There was no compounding effect, no sense of building something cumulative. She was posting into a void that reset every forty-eight hours.

"I'd sit in my apartment in the 11th arrondissement at night, writing these posts, wondering if anyone actually cared," she told me over video call last month. "My colleagues in San Francisco and London had thousands of followers. I had 800.

Maybe it's because I'm French, I thought. Maybe LinkedIn is just an American thing."

Then, during her lunch break at a café near her office, scrolling through LinkedIn while eating a croque-monsieur, she discovered LinkedIn's newsletter feature.

She saw an HR leader in Amsterdam who had 5,000 newsletter subscribers. Another in Berlin with 8,000. They were building audiences that actually grew.

Sophie went back to her office and spent her afternoon researching how newsletters worked.

That evening, she launched "Culture Conversations" (she considered "Conversations sur la Culture" but decided English would reach a broader audience)—a monthly deep-dive on one workplace culture topic, written from her unique perspective bridging French workplace philosophy with global tech culture.

Her first newsletter had forty-seven subscribers (mostly friends and colleagues who wanted to support her).

She almost gave up after that first issue.

"Forty-seven people," she said. "I spent six hours writing it. That's eight minutes per subscriber. I thought: this is ridiculous."

But something different happened over the following months.

Each month, her subscriber count grew: **47 → 134 → 287 → 512 → 891.**

After six months, she had 2,400 subscribers—people who'd explicitly chosen to receive her insights, who got notified every time she published.

When she released her seventh newsletter, it reached those 2,400 people automatically. She didn't have to hope the algorithm would show it to them. They'd already opted in.

The impact cascaded: her newsletter drove profile views, which drove connection requests, which drove speaking invitations.

People started recognizing her name. "Oh, you write Culture Conversations! I read your piece on work-life boundaries last month. It completely changed how I'm managing my team."

Twelve months after launching her newsletter, Sophie was invited to keynote HR Tech Europe in Paris—a conference she'd attended as a participant for years.

The organizer's email said: *"We've been reading Culture Conversations for six months. Your perspective on European workplace culture in the context of global tech is exactly what our audience needs to hear."*

Sophie read that email three times, sitting at her desk in her Paris office, before she fully believed it.

What changed?

Not her expertise. Not her insights. Not her consistency.

What changed was she started using LinkedIn as a platform, not just a feed.

She moved from posting to publishing. From broadcasting to building. From hoping for reach to creating owned channels.

This chapter shows you how to do the same—through features, formats, and tools that amplify your presence beyond individual posts.

Why Features Matter More Than Ever

Most professionals use LinkedIn like a basic text editor: write a post, hit publish, hope it performs.

But LinkedIn has evolved into something far more sophisticated—a full publishing platform with features designed to help you build owned audiences, deepen community, and create compounding reach.

The data backs this up:

- **184,000+ newsletters** published on LinkedIn with engagement up 47% year-over-year

- **100 million+ users** engage with LinkedIn Groups each month

- **500 million+ professionals** subscribed to 146,000+ newsletters (over 3× growth in 18 months)

- **Multi-image posts and native documents** lead engagement: 6.60% for carousels, 6.10% for documents (versus 3–4% for standard posts)

Translation: The professionals who master LinkedIn's features gain disproportionate reach compared to those who only post text.

Sophie's newsletter subscribers became her owned audience—people she could reach consistently, regardless of what the algorithm decided that day.

That's leverage. That's compounding. That's how you move from invisible to influential.

"The difference between posts and newsletters is like the difference between renting and owning," Sophie said. "With posts, you're at the mercy of the algorithm. With newsletters, you build an asset that grows every month."

The Core LinkedIn Features (And How to Use Them Strategically)

Feature 1: LinkedIn Newsletters (Your Owned Audience)

What it is:

A hybrid between LinkedIn posts and email. When you publish a newsletter, subscribers get notified. It appears in feeds AND in their LinkedIn inbox. You build a subscriber base that compounds over time.

Why it matters:

Every post starts from zero reach. A newsletter starts from your subscriber count—**guaranteed distribution.**

When to use it:

If you have a content pillar you want to go deeper on, launch a newsletter around it.

Sophie's approach:

Content pillar: "Bridging European workplace culture with global tech expectations"

Newsletter: "Culture Conversations" (monthly deep-dive)

Her first three topics:

1. "Why the French 35-hour work week makes better leaders (not lazier ones)"
2. "What Silicon Valley can learn from European labor protections"

3. "The Right to Disconnect: How French law changed how I think about boundaries"

"I almost didn't publish that first one," Sophie admitted. "I thought: Americans will think I'm advocating for laziness. But the response was incredible. People were hungry for a different perspective."

How to launch (Sophie's step-by-step process):

1. **Choose one content pillar** (not five—focus)

   Sophie chose: European workplace culture in tech

2. **Pick a cadence you can sustain** (monthly works for most professionals)

   Sophie chose monthly because:
   - She could write 2,000–3,000 words per month sustainably
   - Monthly meant each issue could be comprehensive
   - Subscribers wouldn't feel overwhelmed

3. **Write your first three issues before launching** (proves to yourself you can maintain it)

   "This saved me," Sophie said. "If I'd launched with just one issue written, I would have panicked when month two came around."

4. **Promote in your regular posts**

   "I'm launching a monthly newsletter on European workplace culture in tech. First issue drops next week—subscribe to Culture Conversations."

5. **Deliver consistent value** (every issue should teach something actionable)

   Sophie's rule: Every issue must include:
   - One big idea
   - Three actionable takeaways
   - One story that makes it memorable

What makes newsletters work:

✓ **Specificity:** "Leadership Lessons" is vague. "Leading Remote Teams Across European Timezones" is specific.

✓ **Consistency:** Monthly beats "whenever I feel like it." Your audience learns when to expect you.

✓ **Depth over breadth:** Newsletters allow 3,000+ words. Go deeper than a post can.

✓ **Subscriber growth mindset:** Each issue should make subscribers want to share it.

Sophie's newsletter growth:

Months 1–3: Grew mostly through her existing network (47 → 287)

Months 4–6: Started getting shared by subscribers to their networks (287 → 891)

Months 7–12: Featured in a LinkedIn "Newsletters to Follow" roundup
  (891 → 2,400)

Year 2: Now at 4,200 subscribers

"Every month, I get messages from people saying they shared an issue with their entire team," Sophie said. "That's when I knew it was working—when subscribers became advocates."

Sophie's advice for first-time newsletter creators:

"Start small. Don't try to compete with people who have 50,000 subscribers. Focus on making each issue valuable for the 47 people who believed in you from day one. Growth will come."

Feature 2: LinkedIn Groups (Niche Community Access)

What it is:

Communities organized around specific topics, industries, or interests. 100 million+ users engage in Groups monthly.

Why it matters:

Groups give you access to targeted audiences beyond your immediate network. They're also less algorithm-dependent—group posts go directly to members.

How to use Groups strategically:

Phase 1: Join strategically (Month 1)

Find three to five groups aligned with your content pillars:

- Search for groups in your industry/function

- Look for active groups (posts in the last week)

- Join groups where your ideal audience congregates

Sophie's groups:

1. HR Strategy Leaders Europe (4,800 members)

2. Future of Work—Global (12,000 members)

3. Tech HR Professionals (8,500 members)

4. French Tech Community (6,200 members)

Phase 2: Observe (Months 1–2)

Don't start posting immediately. Watch:

- What topics generate discussion?

- What tone works in this group?

- Who are the most engaged members?

- What questions keep coming up?

"I spent two months just reading," Sophie said. "I noticed the same questions about managing remote teams kept appearing. That became content for my newsletter."

Phase 3: Contribute value (Months 2–6)

Start adding value:

- Answer questions thoughtfully

- Share relevant insights (not self-promotion)

- Ask good questions that spark discussion

- Connect people who can help each other

Sophie's approach:

She set a rule: **Answer three questions per week in her groups.**

"Every Monday morning with my coffee, I'd spend 20 minutes answering questions in my groups. It wasn't about promoting my newsletter. It was about genuinely helping people."

Phase 4: Lead (Month 6+)

Once you're established as a valuable contributor:

- Start discussions around your expertise

- Share your content (but sparingly—add value 5:1 versus self-promotion)

- Consider starting your own group if you identify a gap

Sophie's results:

By month 4, when she shared her newsletter in groups, people subscribed because they already valued her contributions.

"The key is: I helped people for months before I ever mentioned my newsletter. When I finally did share it, they trusted me."

FEATURE 3: LinkedIn Events (Gather Your Community)

What it is:

Create virtual or in-person events, invite attendees, post updates in the event feed, access attendee analytics.

Why it matters:

Events create multiple touchpoints: pre-event promotion, day of engagement, post-event follow-up. Each touchpoint amplifies visibility.

When to use events:

- Virtual lunch and learns (thirty-to-forty-five-minute sessions on your expertise)

- Panel discussions (you +two to three colleagues discussing a topic)

- Q&A sessions (invite your network to ask questions about your domain)

- Community gatherings (informal conversations on themes you care about)

How to maximize event impact:

Before the event (two to three weeks out):

- Create the event with clear value proposition

- Post two to three teasers in the event feed

- Invite your network + relevant groups

- Share the event in your regular posts

Day of the event:

- Post "We're live!" update in event feed

- Engage with attendees in chat/comments

- Capture key quotes or insights to share later

After the event:

- Post highlights as a carousel or summary post

- Thank attendees publicly

- Share recordings or key takeaways

- Convert insights into newsletter content

Sophie's quarterly event: "Culture Conversations Live"

Format: Forty-five-minute virtual discussion on one workplace culture topic

Her first event (Month 6):

- Topic: "Work-Life Boundaries in Always-On Tech Culture"

- Attendees: Forty-three people

- Sophie's feeling: Terrified

"I almost canceled it," she said. "I thought: what if no one shows up? What if my English isn't good enough for a live discussion? What if people think my perspective is too European, too out of touch?"

But forty-three people showed up. They asked questions. They shared their own experiences. The conversation ran fifteen minutes over because people didn't want to leave.

Sophie's event growth:

- Event 1: 43 attendees

- Event 2: 67 attendees

- Event 3: 89 attendees

- Event 4: 112 attendees

The compounding effect:

Each event:

- Drove 60–100 profile views

- Generated 20–30 connection requests

- Created content she repurposed into posts and newsletters

- Built relationships with attendees who became advocates

"After the third event, attendees started bringing their colleagues," Sophie said. "That's when I knew I'd built something real—when people invited others to join."

Feature 4: Long-Form Articles (Establish Depth)

What it is:

LinkedIn's native article publishing platform (up to 125,000 characters versus 3,000 for posts).

When to use:

When a topic deserves deep exploration that a post can't contain.

Strategic use:

1–2× per quarter maximum (don't replace regular posts with articles—use both strategically)

Best practices:

✓ **Compelling headline** (80% of readers never get past it)

✓ **Strong opening hook** (first paragraph determines if they keep reading)

✓ **Subheadings for scannability** (break up long sections)

✓ **Promote via post** (publish article, then share a teaser post linking to it)

Sophie's approach:

She wrote **two to three articles per year**—comprehensive guides that became reference pieces her audience bookmarked and shared.

Her most successful article:

"A Practical Guide to the European Right to Disconnect: What Tech Leaders Need to Know"

- 8,000+ views

- 340 reactions

- 67 comments

- Shared by HR leaders across Europe

- Led to 3 consulting inquiries

"I spent two weeks on that article," Sophie said. "Research, interviews with lawyers, case studies. But it became the thing people associated with my name. Worth every hour."

Feature 5: Polls (Invite Participation)

What it is:

Quick surveys with two to four answer options.

Why they work:

- Low barrier to engagement (one click versus writing a comment)

- Creates curiosity (people want to see results)

- Generates data you can share in follow-up posts

Strategic use:

- Ask genuine questions you're curious about

- Use results to inform future content

- Follow up with insights: *"Last week I polled about X. Here's what the results revealed . . ."*

Caution: Don't overuse. One poll per month maximum or they lose impact.

Sophie's poll strategy:

She runs one poll per quarter, always tied to her newsletter topics.

Example poll:

"How does your company handle after-hours emails?"

- Discouraged but not enforced (48%)

- Formally prohibited (18%)

- No policy (34%)

She used the results in her next newsletter: *"I polled 342 professionals about after-hours emails. Here's what the data reveals about our collective struggle with boundaries . . ."*

Essential Tools That Multiply Your Efficiency

Features are LinkedIn's built-in amplifiers. Tools are what help you use those features consistently without burning out.

Tool Category 1: Visual Design

Canva (Most Essential)

What it does: Create carousels, graphics, banners, social media images

Why employees need it:

- Pre-made LinkedIn templates (carousel, single image, banner)

- Drag-and-drop simple enough for non-designers

- Free version covers 90% of needs

Sophie's workflow:

Sunday evening routine:

- Opens Canva

- Creates one to two carousel templates for the week

- Designs newsletter header image

- Designs event banners

- **Total time:** Forty-five minutes

"I'm not a designer," Sophie said. "But Canva makes me look like one. My content looks professional, which makes people take it seriously."

Tool Category 2: Content Planning and Scheduling

Why scheduling matters:

Consistency requires planning. You won't post weekly for a year if you're deciding what to write every Tuesday morning.

Options:

Taplio/Shield/Hootsuite

- Schedule posts in advance

- Analyze performance

- Track engagement patterns

Simple alternative: Notion + Google Calendar

- Plan content themes monthly

- Write two to three posts ahead

- Schedule writing time, not just posting time

Sophie's system:

Monthly planning (first Sunday of each month):

- Reviews last month's analytics

- Plans four post topics aligned with content pillars

- Outlines newsletter theme

- Blocks two hours every Sunday for content creation

Weekly execution:

- Writes two to three posts every Sunday

- Schedules them for Tuesday 9 AM and Thursday 9 AM (Paris time)

- Frees her mental energy for engagement, not creation

"Planning in batches changed everything," Sophie said. "I'm not staring at a blank screen every Tuesday morning. The content is ready. I just hit publish."

Tool Category 3: AI Writing Assistants

ChatGPT/Claude/Jasper/Writesonic   What they're good for:

✓ Brainstorming post angles

✓ Drafting initial outlines

✓ Reformatting content (post → carousel → newsletter)

✓ Overcoming blank page syndrome

✓ Translation help (Sophie uses for French → English)

What they're NOT good for:

✘ Writing in your voice (requires heavy editing)

✘ Adding personal stories (only you have these)

✘ Creating authentic connection (AI sounds generic)

Sophie's AI workflow:

1. **Brainstorm:** "Give me 10 angles on 'building psychological safety in remote teams across European timezones'"

2. **Review AI suggestions** and pick one to two that resonate

3. **Write the post herself** using her stories, voice, insights

4. **(Optional) Polish:** "Make this more concise" or "Check my English grammar"

Critical rule: AI is a tool, not a replacement. Your voice, stories, and insights must come through.

"I use AI to help with my English," Sophie said. "French is my first language, so I'll ask AI: 'Does this sentence sound natural to a native English speaker?' But the ideas? The stories? Those are mine."

Tool Category 4: Analytics

LinkedIn's Native Analytics (Free)

- Post impressions, engagement rate, demographics

- Newsletter open rates, subscriber growth

- Profile views, search appearances

Third-Party Tools (Paid):

- **Shield:** Deeper analytics, content planning

- **Taplio:** Performance tracking, competitor analysis

What to track:

- ✓ Engagement rate (not just likes—comments, saves, shares)

- ✓ Subscriber growth (for newsletters)

- ✓ Profile views (leading indicator of growing visibility)

- ✓ Content patterns (which topics/formats perform best)

Sophie checks analytics monthly:

First Sunday of each month, with coffee:

- Which newsletter issues got highest open rates?

- Which event had best attendance?

- Which posts drove most profile views?

- Then adjusts strategy based on data

"I track three metrics obsessively," Sophie said:

1. **Newsletter open rate** (goal: above 40%)

2. **Subscriber growth** (goal: 200+ new subscribers per month)

3. **Event attendance rate** (goal: 60% of registrants show up)

"Everything else is noise. These three tell me if I'm building something real."

12 Settings and Security: Protecting Your Brand

The Notification That Changed Everything

On a Tuesday morning, Wei Lin Tan's manager called her into a meeting.

"I noticed you've been updating your LinkedIn profile quite a bit lately," he said, pulling up his phone. "Three times in the last two weeks."

Wei Lin's stomach dropped.

She'd been quietly exploring new opportunities—updating her headline, refining her experience section, and adding recent projects to her featured work. Nothing aggressive. Just . . . positioning herself.

She thought she'd been discreet.

She wasn't.

Every time she updated her profile, LinkedIn sent a notification to her entire network: "Wei Lin updated her profile."

Her manager. Her teammates. Her company's VP. All received automatic broadcasts announcing that something had changed on her profile.

He wasn't accusing her of anything. But the message was clear: "We're watching. And we noticed."

That uncomfortable conversation could have been avoided with one settings change that took thirty seconds.

Later that evening, Wei Lin called her friend Sarah, who worked in tech recruiting.

"I feel so stupid," Wei Lin said. "I thought I was being careful. Turns out I was broadcasting every single change to everyone."

Sarah laughed—not unkindly. "You're not stupid. You just didn't know the settings. Most people don't. Let me show you what to change."

This chapter isn't about paranoia. It's about professional control.

Your LinkedIn presence is powerful—but default settings aren't optimized for employees building their brand while employed. They're optimized for LinkedIn's business model: maximum visibility, maximum engagement, and maximum data collection.

You need to take back control.

Why Default Settings Aren't Your Friend

LinkedIn's default settings assume you want maximum visibility at all times.

Every profile update? Broadcast to your network.

Every profile view? Leaves your digital fingerprint.

Your email, phone number, connections? Visible to anyone who clicks your profile.

Your data? Available for advertising, research, and AI training.

For someone building a personal brand while employed, these defaults create problems:

Problem 1: Unwanted Visibility

Your manager gets notified every time you update your profile—making career exploration awkward.

Problem 2: Loss of Research Privacy

When you view a competitor's profile or a potential employer's page, they see your name—revealing your interests.

Problem 3: Data Overexposure

Your contact information, connections, and activity are more visible than you realize—to recruiters, competitors, and strangers.

Problem 4: Security Vulnerabilities

Without proper protection, your account is one phishing attack away from being compromised—and your professional reputation with it.

The stakes are real:

- **90% of employers review social media profiles** before hiring or promotion decisions (CareerBuilder, 2023)

- **70% of professionals say a colleague's online behavior affects their perception** of that person at work (PwC, 2024)

- LinkedIn has been fined by regulators for data handling practices

- Account hijacking can destroy professional reputation overnight

Your settings aren't just about privacy. They're about professional control.

The Six Critical Settings Areas

Area 1: Profile Visibility and Public Presence

What it controls: Who can see your profile and how much they can see.

Default setting: Maximum public visibility (anyone can see your full profile, including search engines)

Why this matters:

You want to be discoverable—but on your terms. You might want recruiters to find you, but not reveal every detail to random strangers or competitors.

How to optimize:

Settings → Visibility → Edit your public profile

Choose what appears in your public profile (visible to everyone, even non-LinkedIn users):

- ✓ **Keep public:** Photo, headline, current position, summary

- ✓ **Consider hiding:** Full work history, connections, recommendations (keep these for logged-in LinkedIn users only)

Settings → Visibility → Profile viewing options

Choose who can see your full profile:

- **LinkedIn members** (most common for professionals)
- **Your connections only** (if you're very private)
- **Everyone** (maximum discoverability, some privacy trade-off)

Wei Lin's fix:

After her manager's comment (and Sarah's tutorial), she kept her profile public to LinkedIn members (discoverable by recruiters) but hid her connections list (so current employer couldn't see she was connecting with competitors).

Area 2: Activity Broadcasts and Notifications

What it controls: Whether your network gets notified when you update your profile.

Default setting: ON—every update broadcasts to your network

Why this matters:

This is what caught Wei Lin. Every profile tweak sent alerts to her entire network, including her manager.

How to optimize:

Settings → Visibility → Share profile updates with your network → **Toggle OFF**

Once disabled, you can update your profile freely without broadcasting changes.

Critical timing:

- ✓ **Turn this OFF before job searching**
- ✓ **Turn this OFF before major profile updates**
- ✓ **Turn it back ON when you want to announce something** (new role, promotion, achievement)

Wei Lin's second fix:

She turned off profile broadcasts **before** refining her positioning. Once she accepted a new role, she turned broadcasts back on to announce the transition.

Area 3: Profile Viewing Options (Who Knows You Looked)

What it controls: Whether people see your name when you view their profiles.

Default setting: Your name and headline show up when you view someone's profile

Why this matters:

Sometimes you want to research competitors, explore potential employers, or check on former colleagues—without leaving a trace.

The trade-off:

If you browse privately, you also **lose** the ability to see who viewed your profile.

How to optimize:

Settings → Visibility → Profile viewing options

Three options:

1. **Your name and headline** (default)
   - People see exactly who you are when you view their profile
   - You get full "Who viewed your profile" insights
   - **Best for:** Active networking, when you want to be noticed

2. **Private profile characteristics** (semi-anonymous)
   - People see your industry and title, but not your name
   - You get limited "Who viewed your profile" insights
   - **Best for:** Balanced privacy

3. **Private mode** (fully anonymous)
   - No one sees you viewed their profile
   - You get ZERO "Who viewed your profile" insights
   - **Best for:** Research without traces (competitors, potential employers, job searching)

Strategic use:

Wei Lin keeps her default on "Your name and headline" for everyday use—she wants people to see her presence.

But when exploring specific companies while employed, she switches to Private mode temporarily, then switches back.

Pro tip: You can toggle this setting before each browsing session—it's not permanent.

Area 4: Contact Information Visibility

What it controls: Who can see your email, phone number, and other contact details.

Default setting: More visible than you'd expect

Why this matters:

You might want recruiters to contact you—but not random salespeople or strangers.

How to optimize:

Settings → Visibility → Edit your public profile → Contact info

For each item (email, phone, address):

Visibility options:

- **Only you** (most private)
- **Your connections** (1st-degree only)
- **Your network** (first + second degree)
- **Everyone** (including non-LinkedIn users)

Wei Lin's approach:

- **Email:** Visible to first-degree connections (allows networking, blocks spam)
- **Phone:** Only visible to me (I'll share when needed)
- **LinkedIn messaging:** Open to everyone (professional communication channel)

This balance made her reachable for opportunities without opening floodgates to spam.

Area 5: Data Privacy and Third-Party Use

What it controls: How LinkedIn uses your data for advertising, research, and AI training.

Default setting: Maximum data sharing enabled

Why this matters:

LinkedIn monetizes your data. They use it for targeted ads, share it with advertisers, and (in some regions) use your content to train AI models.

You can't opt out of everything—but you can limit some uses.

How to optimize:

Settings → Data privacy

Review and adjust:

- ☐ **Advertising preferences** → Limit ad targeting based on your activity
- ☐ **Data for research** → Opt out where possible (varies by jurisdiction)
- ☐ **Third-party data sharing** → Limit how your data is shared with advertisers
- ☐ **Data for Generative AI Improvement** → Opt out if available in your region (EU, UK, Switzerland have stronger opt-out rights)

Reality check:

You can't completely stop LinkedIn from using your data—that's part of using a free platform. But you can reduce unnecessary sharing.

Wei Lin's stance:

She opted out of research data sharing and limited ad personalization—not because she's paranoid, but because she controls her data choices when possible.

Area 6: Security and Account Protection

What it controls: Who can access your account and how it's protected.

Default setting: Password-only protection (weak)

Why this matters:

If your account is compromised:

- Your professional reputation is at risk

- Hijackers can impersonate you

- Your network becomes vulnerable

- Recovery is time-consuming and embarrassing

How to optimize:

Settings → Account preferences → Two-step verification → Enable

This requires:

1. Your password (something you know)

2. A code sent to your phone (something you have)

Even if someone steals your password, they can't access your account without your phone.

Additional security checks:

☐ **Where you're signed in** → Review active sessions, log out unknown devices

☐ **Recognized devices** → Remove old devices you no longer use

☐ **Change password regularly** → Every six to twelve months

☐ **Use unique password** → Don't reuse passwords from other accounts

Wei Lin's security:

Two-step verification enabled. Password manager for strong, unique passwords. Reviews active sessions quarterly.

One Friday afternoon, she got an alert: "Someone tried to log in from Romania."

Two-step verification blocked it. Without it, her account could have been hijacked.

The Balancing Act: Visibility Versus Privacy

Here's the nuance most people miss:

The goal isn't to hide. It's to appear intentionally.

You're building a professional brand. You want to be discovered by the right people. You want recruiters to find you. You want to demonstrate thought leadership.

But you also want control:

- Control over who sees what

- Control over when updates broadcast

- Control over who tracks your browsing

- Control over your data usage

- Control over your account security

Think of your LinkedIn presence as a professional window you control.

You choose what people see when they look in. Settings give you the curtains, shutters, and blinds.

You don't need to slam the window closed. Just make sure the view aligns with your story and your goals.

Wei Lin's final balance:

✓ **Profile:** Public to LinkedIn members (discoverable)

✓ **Broadcasts:** Turned off while job searching, on when ready to announce

✓ **Browsing:** Private mode only when researching sensitive targets

✓ **Contact info:** Email to connections, phone private

✓ **Data:** Opted out where possible

✓ **Security:** Two-step verification always enabled

This balance let her build her brand publicly while maintaining privacy about her career exploration—until she was ready to make it public.

The Ten-Minute Settings Audit (Do This Now)

Take ten minutes right now to optimize your settings:

Minutes 1–2: Profile broadcasts

☐ Turn off "Share profile updates with your network" (unless you're actively announcing something)

Minutes 3–4: Contact info

☐ Set email visibility to "Connections only"

☐ Set phone to "Only you" (share manually when needed)

Minutes 5–6: Profile viewing

☐ Keep default on "Your name and headline" for now

☐ Know how to switch to Private mode when needed

Minutes 7–8: Data privacy

☐ Opt out of research data sharing

☐ Limit ad personalization

☐ Opt out of AI training if available in your region

Minutes 9–10: Security

☐ Enable two-step verification

☐ Review active sessions, remove unknown devices

☐ Update password if it's been >12 months

Done.

Ten minutes to protect years of brand building.

Common Scenarios and Solutions

Scenario 1: Quietly exploring new opportunities while employed

Settings to adjust:

✓ Turn off profile update broadcasts

✓ Use private browsing when viewing target companies

- ✓ Limit who can see your connections (so current employer doesn't see you connecting with competitors)
- ✓ Keep profile public to LinkedIn members (so recruiters can find you)

Scenario 2: Building thought leadership publicly

Settings to adjust:

- ✓ Profile public to maximize discoverability
- ✓ Broadcasts ON (you want people notified of updates)
- ✓ Contact info visible to connections (for collaboration opportunities)
- ✓ Default profile viewing (you want your name visible when networking)

Scenario 3: Taking a break but keeping profile active

Settings to adjust:

- ✓ Turn off broadcasts (no notifications when you update)
- ✓ Private browsing if you're checking in occasionally
- ✓ Keep security tight even when not active

Scenario 4: Announcing a major career move

Settings to adjust:

- ✓ Turn broadcasts back ON before updating with new role
- ✓ Profile fully public (maximize visibility of achievement)
- ✓ Update contact info if transitioning (new email, etc.)

V Community—From Connections to Relationships

Building a presence on LinkedIn isn't about collecting followers; it's about cultivating trust-based relationships. A strong professional community can open doors, amplify your ideas, and build credibility that algorithms alone can't manufacture. Real networking on LinkedIn isn't transactional, it's relational. This section explores the principles that transform connections into community, and how to build trust that compounds over time.

13 The Five Pillars of Trust: How to Build Credibility That Lasts

The Product Manager Nobody Expected

Sarah Chen posts on LinkedIn every Tuesday morning at 7:15 AM.

She's not a CEO. She's not an influencer. She doesn't have an MBA from Stanford or a title that opens doors. She's a mid-level product manager at a software company most people have never heard of in Denver, Colorado.

And yet.

When Sarah posts about the mundane realities of product development—the failed launches, the miscommunications with engineering, the small victories in user research—something remarkable happens.

People listen.

Her posts reach somewhere between 50,000 and 70,000 people. Her followers include VPs at Fortune 500 companies, startup founders, and college students trying to break into tech. When she shares a framework, people save it. When she asks a question, people answer thoughtfully. When she admits a mistake, the comments fill with gratitude: "Thank you for being honest about this."

Sarah has become what we might call a trusted voice.

But here's what makes her story interesting: five years ago, she had 200 connections and posted maybe twice a year. Her content got three likes—from her college roommate, her brother, and one very supportive colleague.

"I thought LinkedIn was fake," she told me over coffee last month. "All these people humble-bragging about their promotions and posting motivational quotes over sunsets. I didn't see myself in any of it."

So what changed?

Sarah Chen didn't become smarter. She didn't get a better job title. She didn't hire a personal branding consultant.

What she did was figure out—partly by accident, partly by observation—the fundamental mechanics of trust on LinkedIn.

And trust, it turns out, follows rules.

This chapter breaks down those rules into five pillars. Master them, and you don't need to be a CEO to build credibility that compounds.

Pillar 1: Consistency the Power of Showing Up

In 2019, researchers at LinkedIn's data science division noticed something curious.

They were studying engagement patterns—who got seen, who got ignored, who managed to break through the noise. What they discovered contradicted almost everything the platform's engineers had assumed about virality.

The people who succeeded weren't the ones who posted most frequently. They weren't the ones with the cleverest headlines or the most aggressive hashtag strategies.

The winners, statistically speaking, were people who simply showed up—regularly, predictably, with a recognizable voice.

Consistency is the first pillar of trust.

Think about what consistency actually signals. When you encounter someone who posts every Thursday morning, who maintains a recognizable tone and focus, your brain makes a calculation.

It's the same calculation you make when you see a restaurant that's been in business for thirty years, or a friend who always calls on your birthday.

You think: This person is reliable. This person takes their reputation seriously. This person can be trusted.

LinkedIn's own data bear this out: Creators who maintain a weekly posting rhythm receive 3× the visibility of those who post sporadically.

But here's what's interesting: the algorithm isn't rewarding frequency for frequency's sake. It's rewarding predictability. The platform has learned what humans have always known—that trust begins with pattern recognition.

Sarah's Discovery

Sarah stumbled into this by accident.

In early 2020, she'd just finished a particularly brutal product launch. Everything that could go wrong had gone wrong. The engineering team had missed deadlines. Marketing had misunderstood the value proposition. The CEO had unexpectedly announced features that didn't exist yet at a board meeting.

Exhausted and frustrated, Sarah wrote a LinkedIn post on a Tuesday morning while eating toast at her kitchen table. It wasn't polished. It wasn't strategic. It was just honest.

"Here's what happens when a product launch goes sideways," she wrote. Then she listed the five things her team had learned the hard way.

The post got 200 reactions and 30 comments—the most engagement she'd ever received.

"I expected people to judge me for admitting failure," she said. "Instead, they thanked me for being real."

The following Tuesday, she posted again. Not because she had a strategy—because she had something to say.

Then the Tuesday after that.

By month three, something strange started happening: people began looking for her posts. She'd get messages: "I missed your Tuesday post this week—everything okay?"

She hadn't set out to build a schedule. But by showing up consistently, she'd inadvertently created an expectation. And meeting that expectation, week after week, became the foundation of everything that followed.

The Consistency Checklist:

✓ Choose a cadence you can sustain (weekly beats sporadic intensity)

✓ Pick a day and time (train your audience when to expect you)

✓ Maintain a consistent voice (your posts should feel like the same person wrote them)

✓ Don't disappear without explanation (even a short break deserves acknowledgment)

✓ Build systems that support showing up (draft posts in advance when life gets busy)

Consistency isn't about perfection. It's about presence.

Sarah still misses occasional Tuesdays—vacations, sick days, overwhelming work weeks. But when she does, she acknowledges it. "Skipped last week because I was underwater with deadlines. Back today with lessons from that chaos."

Her audience doesn't expect perfection. They expect her to keep showing up.

And she does.

Pillar 2: Authenticity the Trust That Comes from Truth

In 2022, the public relations firm Edelman released its annual Trust Barometer—a survey measuring how much people trust various institutions and figures.

The results contained a puzzle that should make every corporate communications department rethink its strategy.

When asked who they trusted most to tell them the truth about a company, respondents ranked "regular employees" significantly higher than CEOs.

Not slightly higher. Significantly higher.

The person sitting in a cubicle on the fourth floor was more credible than the person in the corner office on the top floor.

This is Pillar 2: Authenticity.

The reason for this paradox is simple, though its implications are profound.

CEOs are expected to spin. They're expected to present the company in the best possible light, to smooth over problems, to project confidence even in moments of uncertainty.

We understand this. We discount for it.

But we expect something different from regular employees. We expect them to tell us what's actually happening.

When Sarah Chen writes about a product launch that failed, she's not violating corporate protocol—she's exercising the strange authority that comes from honest disclosure.

When she admits uncertainty, when she shares a lesson learned the hard way, when she writes in her own voice rather than in corporate speak, she's making a claim that's almost impossible for executives to make.

She's saying: I'm telling you the truth.

The Moment Sarah Found Her Voice

For the first year of posting, Sarah tried to sound "professional."

She'd draft posts, then edit out anything that felt too casual or too vulnerable. She'd remove contractions. She'd replace "I was terrified" with "I approached the situation with some uncertainty." She'd scrub out personality in pursuit of polish.

The posts were fine. They got modest engagement. But they didn't connect.

Then one Tuesday, she was running late. She'd drafted a post about roadmap prioritization, but it felt stiff and boring. With ten minutes before her self-imposed 7:15 AM deadline, she scrapped it and wrote this instead:

> "I spent three hours yesterday trying to explain to our VP why we can't build all
> five features he wants by next quarter. I failed. He still thinks we can. I'm tired, I'm
> frustrated, and I honestly don't know if I'm the problem or if he just doesn't
> understand how software development actually works.
>
> Anyone else ever feel like they're speaking a different language than leadership?"

She almost didn't hit publish. It felt too raw. Too complainy. Too unprofessional.

But she was tired, and she was late, and she pressed Post anyway.

Within an hour: 400 reactions. Within two hours: 80 comments.

Product managers from around the world writing: "THIS." "Every week." "I thought it was just me."

Senior leaders writing: "As a VP, I'm guilty of this. Thank you for the reminder to listen better."

One comment stuck with her: "This is the first LinkedIn post I've read in months that sounds like an actual human wrote it."

Sarah stared at that comment for a long time.

She'd spent a year trying to sound professional. One moment of unfiltered honesty generated more genuine connection than anything she'd carefully crafted.

The Authenticity Test

Authenticity on LinkedIn isn't about sharing everything. It's about sharing what's real.

Before Sarah posts now, she asks herself three questions:

1. **Would I say this to a colleague over coffee?** If yes, it's probably authentic. If no, it might be performance.

2. **Am I trying to impress, or am I trying to connect?** Impressive content gets likes. Honest content gets comments and saves.

3. **Does this sound like me, or does it sound like LinkedIn?** If you can't tell who wrote it, neither can your audience.

The mistake many professionals make is thinking they need to sound "professional," which they interpret as formal, polished, corporate.

But professionalism and authenticity aren't opposites. They're complements.

The most effective LinkedIn posts sound like they were written by a thoughtful human being, not a public relations department.

What Authenticity Looks Like:

> ✓ Admitting when you don't have answers
>
> ✓ Sharing lessons from failures, not just successes
>
> ✓ Writing in your actual voice (contractions, casual phrases, personality)
>
> ✓ Acknowledging complexity (the world isn't black and white)
>
> ✓ Being specific about struggles (vague vulnerability isn't vulnerability)

What Authenticity Doesn't Mean:

> ✖ Oversharing personal drama
>
> ✖ Complaining without insight
>
> ✖ Violating confidentiality for clicks
>
> ✖ Using vulnerability as performance art
>
> ✖ Being unprofessional in the name of "keeping it real"

Authenticity is the bridge between credibility and connection.

Sarah learned this the hard way: people don't follow perfect. They follow real.

Pillar 3: Relevance Creating Value Worth Saving

In early 2025, LinkedIn's product team changed how they measured content quality.

For years, the platform had used likes as the primary metric of engagement. Likes are easy to track, easy to understand, and easy to optimize for.

But likes, the data scientists realized, don't actually tell you much about value.

So they started paying attention to a different metric: saves.

When someone saves a post, they're making a statement. They're saying: This is valuable enough that I want to come back to it. This contains information I might need next week, or next month, or in a different context. This is worth keeping.

LinkedIn's 2025 content study found that saves—not likes—are the strongest predictor of long-term audience growth.

A post with 500 likes might generate a brief spike in visibility. But a post with 50 saves creates lasting value. It becomes a resource. It gets shared. It compounds.

This is Pillar 3: Relevance.

Relevance is harder to achieve than virality.

Going viral is about emotion, about triggering an immediate reaction. Relevance is about utility. It's about helping people solve problems, understand complexity, or see familiar situations in new ways.

Sarah's Framework Test

Sarah discovered this through experimentation.

Early in her LinkedIn journey, she'd alternate between two types of posts:

Type 1: Personal stories Narrative posts about her experiences—launches that failed, conversations that went wrong, moments of doubt.

These got good engagement. People connected with the emotion. They'd comment with empathy or share similar experiences.

Type 2: Practical frameworks Posts that broke down how she actually did her job—how to prioritize features, how to run effective user interviews, how to communicate bad news to stakeholders.

These got fewer immediate reactions. But something interesting happened over time.

The framework posts kept getting saved. Weeks after publishing, she'd get messages: "I used your stakeholder communication template in a meeting today. It worked." Or "I bookmarked your post about feature prioritization. Referenced it three times this month."

Sarah ran the numbers. Her personal stories averaged 300 reactions and 5 saves. Her frameworks averaged 150 reactions and 40 saves.

The frameworks were building something the personal stories weren't: lasting value.

She realized: viral moments feel good. But relevant content creates opportunity.

The Relevance Question

Now, before Sarah posts anything, she asks herself:

"Would someone find this valuable enough to save?"

That question changes everything.

It shifts the focus from performance to service. From attention-seeking to value creation. It transforms social media from a vanity project into something more substantial: a way of thinking out loud that actually helps other people think.

What Makes Content Relevant:

- ✓ It solves a problem your audience actually has

- ✓ It provides a framework they can apply tomorrow

- ✓ It breaks down complex ideas into understandable steps

- ✓ It answers questions before they have to ask them

- ✓ It makes them better at their jobs

Red Flags for Irrelevance:

- ✗ You're sharing a motivational quote because you can't think of anything else

- ✗ You're posting about something trending but irrelevant to your expertise

- ✗ You're telling a story with no takeaway or lesson

- ✗ You're writing about what you think will perform, not what your audience needs

- ✗ You can't articulate who this post helps or how

Sarah's most saved post ever (1,200 saves) was titled: "The 3-Question Test I Use Before Every Product Decision."

It wasn't clever. It wasn't emotional. It wasn't even particularly well-written.

But it was immediately useful. Product managers around the world saved it, shared it with their teams, and referenced it in meetings.

That's relevance.

That's the kind of content that builds authority.

Pillar 4: Expertise Demonstrating Knowledge Through Contribution

In 2023, researchers analyzing LinkedIn's engagement patterns discovered something that challenged conventional wisdom about online content.

They found that the posts generating the most meaningful engagement—the ones that led to new connections, job opportunities, and genuine professional relationships—weren't the ones that got the most likes.

They were the ones that kept people reading.

They called this metric "dwell time." How long does someone stay on your post? Do they scroll past in two seconds, or do they actually read it? Do they sit with it? Do they think about it?

Posts that teach had 40–60% higher dwell time than posts that merely announce.

When you show people how to do something, or help them understand why something works the way it does, or share a framework they can apply to their own work—they stay. They learn.

And they remember you.

This is Pillar 4: Expertise.

But here's the critical distinction: expertise on LinkedIn isn't about credentials.

It's about demonstration.

Nobody cares where you went to school or what your job title is. They care about how you think. They care about what you can teach them.

The Day Sarah Stopped Listing Credentials

When Sarah first started posting regularly, she'd begin every post the same way:

"As a Senior Product Manager with 7 years of experience . . ."

She thought credentials mattered. She thought people needed to know she was qualified before they'd listen.

Then she attended a LinkedIn conference where a speaker said something that stuck with her:

"Your resume tells people what you've done. Your content shows them how you think. On LinkedIn, how you think is what matters."

Sarah went home and looked at her most engaged posts. None of them started with credentials. The best ones started with insight:

- "Here's what nobody tells you about roadmap planning . . ."
- "I just watched a product launch fail in real-time. Here's what went wrong . . ."
- "Three questions that change how I prioritize features . . ."

Her expertise emerged through her analysis. Through the way she broke down complex decisions. Through the patterns she'd noticed over years of doing the work.

She didn't declare expertise. She revealed it.

How Expertise Shows Up Authentically:

✓ Breaking down your thought process (not just your conclusions)

✓ Sharing frameworks you've developed (not just ones you've read about)

✓ Analyzing why something worked or didn't work (not just what happened)

✓ Connecting dots others might miss (pattern recognition)

✓ Teaching through examples from your real work (not abstract theory)

What Undermines Perceived Expertise:

✘ Starting posts with "As a [title] . . ." or credential-dropping

✘ Sharing generic advice anyone could Google

✘ Repeating what others have said without adding your perspective

✘ Making sweeping statements without supporting evidence or examples

✘ Positioning yourself as having all the answers (experts acknowledge complexity)

The most effective posts don't declare expertise. They reveal it through the quality of the insight, through the depth of the analysis, and through the usefulness of the framework.

Authority today isn't about position. It's about contribution.

Sarah's posts now read like conversations with a thoughtful colleague—someone who's been in the trenches, learned some things the hard way, and wants to help you avoid the same mistakes.

That's more valuable than any job title.

Pillar 5: Empathy the Human Touch That Sustains Connection

There's a final element that separates trusted voices from ignored ones, and it's the one that's easiest to overlook.

LinkedIn's internal analytics team discovered that posts written in a conversational, inclusive tone receive 2× the engagement of posts written in formal corporate language.

This is Pillar 5: Empathy.

Empathy on LinkedIn isn't about being soft or emotional. It's about awareness.

It's about understanding that on the other side of every view, every comment, every connection request, there's another human being trying to navigate their own professional challenges.

Sarah's Comment Section Transformation

For the first few months of consistent posting, Sarah would publish her content and then . . . disappear.

She'd check back later to see the metrics—how many likes, how many comments. But she didn't engage. She didn't respond. She treated comments like feedback on a presentation, not like the beginning of a conversation.

Then one day, a junior product manager left a comment on one of her posts:

"This is helpful, but I'm struggling with something you didn't mention. When stakeholders disagree with each other about priorities, how do you navigate that without making enemies?"

Sarah almost replied with "Great question!" and moved on.

But something made her pause. She remembered being that junior PM. She remembered feeling like everyone else had it figured out except her. She remembered how lonely it felt to be drowning in problems with no one to ask.

So instead, she wrote a three-paragraph response. She shared a specific story about a time she'd handled conflicting stakeholders badly and what she'd learned. She ended with: "This is one of the hardest parts of the job. You're not alone in struggling with it."

The junior PM replied: "Thank you. I've been feeling like I'm failing at something everyone else finds easy. This helps more than you know."

That exchange stayed with Sarah.

She realized: her posts were creating value. But her comments could create connection.

Now, when Sarah responds to comments, she doesn't just thank people for engaging. She actually engages.

She asks follow-up questions. She acknowledges other perspectives. She spotlights colleagues. She writes with humility—talking with her network, not at it.

What Empathy Looks Like in Practice:

- ✓ Responding thoughtfully to comments (not just "Thanks!")
- ✓ Acknowledging different perspectives (not everyone faces the same challenges)
- ✓ Celebrating others' wins in your posts (spotlight colleagues)
- ✓ Admitting when you don't have answers (vulnerability invites dialogue)
- ✓ Making space for disagreement (respectful debate strengthens community)
- ✓ Remembering commenters are people with names (not just engagement metrics)

What Erodes Empathy:

- ✗ Treating your posts as broadcasts instead of invitations
- ✗ Ignoring comments or giving generic "Thanks!" replies

✖ Getting defensive when someone disagrees

✖ Making your content all about you (your wins, your insights, your journey)

✖ Forgetting that junior professionals are watching and learning from how you show up

People remember who made them feel seen.

They remember who treated their questions with respect, who acknowledged their contributions, and who created space for dialogue rather than monologue.

Empathy is the bridge between credibility and connection.

You can have all the consistency, authenticity, relevance, and expertise in the world, but without empathy—without the human touch—you're just another voice in an increasingly crowded space.

The Power of Many Voices: When Individual Trust Becomes Collective Impact

Sarah Chen posts every Tuesday at 7:15 AM.

But she's not the only one anymore.

Three months after Sarah started posting consistently, a junior product manager on her team—someone who'd been quietly watching from the sidelines—sent her a Slack message:

"I read your post this morning about the 3-Question Test. It made me think about something that happened on my project last week. Do you think . . . would it be weird if I wrote about it on LinkedIn?"

Sarah smiled. She remembered that exact hesitation. The fear of being too visible. The worry that nobody would care.

"Not weird at all," she replied. "Do it."

Two weeks later, that colleague posted their first reflection about user research—a small, honest story about discovering a critical insight by actually watching customers use their product instead of relying on surveys.

It got sixty-seven reactions and twelve comments.

More importantly, it sparked a conversation that connected them with a senior UX researcher at another company who later became a mentor.

One voice had inspired another.

And that's when Sarah realized something she hadn't anticipated:

Individual trust compounds. But collective trust multiplies.

From One Voice to Many

For eighteen months, Sarah had been building her presence alone—her voice, her insights, her Tuesday morning ritual.

But her decision to share publicly had created something unexpected: permission.

When her colleagues saw Sarah posting authentically about product management challenges, when they watched her admit failures and share frameworks, when they noticed that vulnerability didn't damage her career but actually enhanced it—they started asking themselves: "Maybe I could do that too?"

Within six months of that first colleague's post, five people on Sarah's team were posting regularly. Each with their own voice. Each with their own perspective. Each contributing to conversations about product management, user research, stakeholder communication, and technical decision-making.

Sarah's director noticed.

Not because it was coordinated—it wasn't. Not because anyone had told them to post—they hadn't. But because suddenly, when clients and partners searched for information about product thinking at their company, they found a chorus of authentic voices instead of silence.

"I didn't realize how invisible we were until we weren't," the director told Sarah over coffee. "Your team just put us on the map."

The New Trust Economy

This is the shift that's quietly transforming professional reputation in 2025.

For years, corporate credibility lived in carefully managed brand messages, polished marketing campaigns, official announcements. The company spoke. The audience listened.

But on LinkedIn, that dynamic has inverted.

According to Nielsen's Consumer Trust Index, 92% of people trust recommendations from individuals—even strangers—over branded messages.

Edelman's Trust Barometer consistently shows that regular employees are trusted more than CEOs when discussing company practices (52% versus 38%).

LinkedIn Marketing Solutions data reveal that content shared by employees receives 561% greater reach than the same content shared by the company page.

And Sprout Social's 2024 research found that 64% of consumers trust a company more when employees share genuine content about their work.

The pattern is unmistakable: trust doesn't flow from logos anymore. It flows through people.

When Sarah posts about product management challenges in Denver, when Priya Sharma (Chapter 8) shares insights about hiring for potential in Mumbai, when Miguel Santos (Chapter 10) documents his framework experiments in Manila—each of those voices builds credibility not just for themselves, but for their organizations.

Collectively, they humanize institutions. They show audiences not just what companies do, but who stands behind them.

Your Voice as Part of a Chorus

If you've been reading this book as an individual employee wondering how your posts matter in the bigger picture, here's what you need to understand:

When you share your learning on LinkedIn, you're not just building your personal brand. You're building something bigger.

You're creating network effects. Your colleague reads your post and gains confidence to share their own perspective. Their post inspires another teammate. Suddenly, your organization has visible expertise in an area that was invisible six months ago.

You're raising all boats. When five people at your company post thoughtful insights, the organization becomes known for that topic. When recruiters search for expertise in your field, they find not one person, but a team.

You're building career insurance. Not job security—opportunity security. When you and your colleagues are all visible on LinkedIn, you're building professional reputations that transcend any single employer. If your company restructures or you decide to move on, you're not starting from zero. You have a network. You have demonstrated expertise. You have relationships built over years of showing up.

You're modeling leadership. Sarah's decision to post every Tuesday didn't just benefit Sarah. It gave her teammates permission to do the same. That's leadership—not because of title or authority, but because of example.

The Collective Amplification

Here's what happened after Sarah's team started posting:

Three months in: The company's recruiting efforts improved. Job candidates mentioned reading employee posts in their cover letters. "I can tell this is a place where people actually think deeply about their work," one candidate wrote.

Six months in: A major client mentioned in a meeting that they'd been following posts from the product team. "We see you're really wrestling with the challenges we're wrestling with. That's why we want to work with you."

Twelve months in: The company's LinkedIn page follower count increased by 3× without any paid promotion. The CEO pulled up Sarah's original post from two years ago in a company-wide meeting: "This is where it started. Sarah didn't ask for permission. She just shared something real. And it changed our company."

None of this was coordinated. There was no employee advocacy program. No mandatory posting schedule. No branded templates.

Just authentic professionals doing meaningful work and sharing what they learned along the way.

The Freedom Within Framework

When Sarah's company saw what was happening organically, HR created a simple one-page guideline:

Encouraged Topics:

- Lessons from your work
- Behind-the-scenes problem-solving
- Professional development insights
- Team collaboration stories
- Industry observations from your role

Off-Limits Topics:

- Confidential client information
- Unreleased product details
- Financial data not yet public
- Internal personnel matters
- Anything that violates your employment agreement

Tone Guidance:

- Be professional, but be yourself
- Share what you learned, not just what you achieved
- Give credit to teammates
- If unsure, ask your manager or HR

That was it. No approval chains. No scripts. Just clarity and trust.

The message was clear: Your voice matters. Use it responsibly. We trust you.

When Trust Compounds Collectively

Remember the five pillars from this chapter:

1. **Consistency**—When multiple people show up regularly, the organization becomes known for sustained thought leadership

2. **Authenticity**—When employees speak in their own voices, the company brand feels human, not corporate

3. **Relevance**—When different team members share practical insights, the organization becomes a go-to resource

4. **Expertise**—When knowledge is visible across many people, the company is seen as having deep bench strength

5. **Empathy**—When employees engage thoughtfully with their networks, the organization builds genuine relationships

Individual trust built through these five pillars doesn't just benefit you. It radiates outward.

Your credibility enhances your colleagues' credibility. Your colleagues' visibility enhances yours. Together, you create something greater than the sum of your individual efforts: a reputation for excellence, authenticity, and expertise.

What This Means for You

You don't need permission to start sharing your learning on LinkedIn.

You don't need to wait for your company to launch an official program.

You don't need a title, a big team, or a marketing budget.

You just need to:

- ✓ **Share what you're learning**—Document your work, reflect on challenges, share frameworks that helped you

- ✓ **Give credit generously**—When you post about team achievements, name your teammates

- ✓ **Invite others in**—When a colleague asks about your LinkedIn presence, share your process

- ✓ **Stay consistent**—Show up regularly, even if it's just once a month

- ✓ **Be authentically yourself**—Don't try to sound corporate; sound like you

When you do these things, you're not just building your personal brand. You're contributing to something bigger: a movement where professionals help each other learn, where companies become visible through their people, where trust is earned collectively.

Sarah's Reflection

Two years after posting her first honest reflection about a failed product launch, Sarah sat in a company meeting where the CEO showed her original post on a big screen.

"This is where it started," he said. "Sarah didn't ask for permission. She didn't wait for a corporate social media policy. She just shared something real. And it changed our company.

Not because it was a brilliant marketing strategy. But because it was authentic. And authenticity is contagious.

So here's what I want to say: If you've been thinking about sharing your work on LinkedIn but you've been hesitating—don't. This company succeeds when your voices are heard. When you share what you're learning, when you document your challenges, when you participate in your professional community—you're not just helping yourself. You're helping all of us."

After the meeting, Sarah's phone buzzed with a LinkedIn message from someone she'd never met—a product manager at another company who'd been following her posts for months.

"I just wanted to say thank you," the message read. "Your posts gave me the courage to start sharing my own work. I posted my first reflection last week, and three people from my team reached out to say it inspired them too.

I think we're all just trying to figure this out together. But it helps to know we're not alone."

Sarah smiled.

That was exactly it.

None of them were alone. They were part of something bigger.

A community of professionals who believed that learning out loud, helping each other, and sharing authentically wasn't just good for careers—it was good for the world.

One voice at a time. One post at a time. One Tuesday morning at a time.

14 Networking on LinkedIn: Building Community, Not Just Connections

The Comment That Changed Everything

On a Wednesday morning in 2019, Carolina Silva sat at her desk in Vila Olímpia, São Paulo's tech district, scrolling through LinkedIn before her 9 AM meeting.

The office was already buzzing—her marketing agency occupied the third floor of a glass tower on Rua Funchal, surrounded by startups, venture capital firms, and the kind of aggressive ambition that defined São Paulo's business scene.

She stopped on a post by someone she'd never met—a product manager at a tech company in California sharing a framework about product roadmaps. Nothing groundbreaking, just someone thinking out loud about their work.

Carolina almost scrolled past. She had a client presentation in twenty minutes. Her coffee was getting cold. Her manager was already in the conference room setting up.

But something in the post resonated. Her team had tried something similar six months ago—a product launch for a Brazilian e-commerce client. They'd learned things the hard way.

She left a comment: three sentences about what they'd learned, what worked, what didn't. Specific. Based on real experience. No fluff.

Ninety seconds of her time. Then she closed LinkedIn and went to her meeting.

The author replied an hour later. Carolina replied back during lunch at a nearby restaurante, sitting outside in the São Paulo sun. Three comments total. Then the conversation ended naturally.

Carolina didn't think about it again.

Two years later, that same person introduced Carolina to the VP who would eventually hire her to lead marketing for a US company's Latin American operations.

He didn't remember the specific post. He couldn't even recall the exact framework they'd discussed.

But he remembered her name.

Because after that first exchange, Carolina had continued showing up.

Not in his inbox with aggressive pitches. Not with awkward connection requests asking for favors. Not with self-promotional posts trying to get his attention.

But in the comments.

On his posts. On posts they both engaged with. In the conversations happening at the intersection of their professional worlds—product marketing, Latin American tech ecosystems, cross-border growth strategies.

Over two years, they'd probably exchanged thirty comments total across a dozen different conversations. Never more than a few sentences at a time. Never forced. Always adding value.

By the time they actually met on a video call—Carolina in her Vila Olímpia apartment, him in San Francisco—they weren't strangers. They were already part of the same community.

He knew how she thought. She understood his perspective. The trust was already there.

When the VP asked him if he knew anyone who could lead LATAM marketing, Carolina's name came up immediately.

"She gets it," he said. "She's been part of our conversations for two years. She understands both US tech culture and Latin American markets. She's the person."

In São Paulo's competitive professional scene—where everyone was hustling, building personal brands, trying to stand out—Carolina had learned something most professionals miss:

Visibility isn't about being loud. It's about being present.

This Is How LinkedIn Actually Works

Not through perfectly crafted posts that go viral.

Not through connection requests to strangers hoping they'll open doors.

Not through broadcasting your achievements to an audience of thousands.

But through the quiet, consistent accumulation of micro-interactions that build recognition, trust, and, eventually, opportunity.

The difference between having connections and building community is the difference between collecting business cards and cultivating relationships.

One is a transaction. The other is a transformation.

Carolina's reflection:

"I didn't have a networking strategy," she told me over video call from her apartment in Pinheiros, São Paulo's creative neighborhood. "I just showed up where interesting conversations were happening. I added my perspective when I had something to say. I was helpful without expecting anything back.

Two years later, opportunities found me. Not because I was trying to network—because I was part of a community."

From Rolodex to Ecosystem

Most people treat LinkedIn like a digital Rolodex—a place to store contact information for people they might need someday.

The most successful professionals understand something different: LinkedIn is an ecosystem of continuous value exchange.

A connection is a click. A community is a conversation.

Harvard Business Review research shows that professionals who engage consistently in "micro-interactions"—short, authentic exchanges online—experience stronger career mobility and more mentorship opportunities than those who only post updates.

LinkedIn's own data confirms this pattern: members who comment meaningfully receive 5× more profile views and 7× more connection requests over time compared to those who only post or scroll passively.

More striking: comments drive 30–75× more views than likes.

Read that again: thirty to seventy-five times more visibility.

That means a single thoughtful comment on the right post can generate more reach than a dozen posts to your own feed. Posts that spark meaningful comment threads see up to 2.4× higher reach compared to posts with fewer interactions.

Network science research confirms what experienced LinkedIn users already know intuitively: maintaining even weak ties through the platform significantly boosts professional opportunities. One study found that a 10-percentile improvement in network connectivity corresponded to a 0.27-percentile increase in monthly recruiter InMails.

Translation: the strength of your network directly predicts the opportunities that find you.

But here's what that data doesn't capture—and what Carolina understood instinctively:

Networks aren't built through strategy. They're built through showing up.

The Foundation: LinkedIn Etiquette That Builds Trust

Before we talk about what to do, let's establish what not to do.

Imagine attending a networking event where someone:

✖ Hands you their business card, then immediately walks away

✖ Talks about themselves for ten minutes without asking you a single question

✘ Asks for a job referral within thirty seconds of meeting you

✘ Corners the keynote speaker to pitch their startup

You'd think they were tone-deaf. Maybe even rude.

Yet on LinkedIn, these behaviors happen constantly.

The "Would You Do This in Real Life?" test is your filter. Before you send that message, leave that comment, or make that request, ask yourself:

Would I do this at an in-person networking event?

If the answer is no, don't do it online.

Digital etiquette isn't about following arbitrary rules. It's about recognizing that people on the other side of the screen are still people—with limited time, their own priorities, and a finely tuned radar for authenticity versus opportunism.

Here's what good LinkedIn etiquette actually looks like:

1. **Acknowledge engagement thoughtfully**
   When someone invests time commenting on your post, respond with intention. Not just "Thanks!" but something that continues the conversation or shows you actually read what they wrote.

2. **Reciprocate effort**
   If someone writes a paragraph-long comment sharing their experience, return one of equal care. If they leave an emoji, a simple acknowledgment works. Small signals reinforce connection.

3. **Understand algorithmic reciprocity**
   Each comment you reply to tells LinkedIn's algorithm that your post is active, which pushes it to second- and third-degree networks. Engagement begets engagement. But don't reply just for the algorithm—reply because someone took time to engage with your work.

4. **Avoid "post and run" behavior**
   The first hour after publishing is crucial. Not because of vanity metrics, but because human attention is freshest and the algorithm is watching how people respond. Set aside twenty to thirty minutes after posting to engage, reply, and spark conversation.

This habit trains both people and algorithms to trust your presence.

Carolina's practice:

"In São Paulo's marketing scene, everyone's posting constantly," she said. "But most people hit 'share' and disappear. I learned early: if you're going to post, stay. Respond to comments. Ask follow-up questions. Turn your post into a conversation, not an announcement."

From Broadcasting to Building

When you post on LinkedIn and walk away, you're broadcasting.

When you comment, connect, reply, and follow up, you're networking.

The difference determines whether your presence creates opportunity or just creates noise.

Here's what the shift looks like in practice:

BEFORE you post your own content, comment on others' posts
   This demonstrates presence and adds value before asking for attention. The algorithm rewards early engagement on fresh content, which means your thoughtful morning comments often get more visibility than your afternoon posts.

RESPOND to every meaningful comment within the first hour
   Not because you're obligated, but because someone took time to engage with your thinking. The algorithm rewards quick, genuine replies. More importantly, your community feels seen.

WHEN you send connection requests, include context
   Reference something specific: a post they wrote, an insight you appreciated, a shared interest you noticed. Treat networking like starting a conversation, not filling out a form.

MAKE "thank you" posts part of your rhythm
   Not just for big wins, but for small collaborations. Spotlight the colleague who helped you solve a problem. Name the person who introduced you to a new idea. These posts show relational depth, not just achievement.

SET a fifteen-minute pre-post ritual

Before you publish your own content, browse your feed and leave three to five thoughtful comments. You warm up your brain, add value to others, and prime the algorithm to pay attention when you do post.

Think of it like arriving early to a party and helping the host set up. When you eventually share your own story, people are already glad you're there.

Carolina's routine:

"Every morning at my Vila Olímpia desk, before I write anything myself, I spend 15 minutes reading and commenting. I call it my 'warm-up'. By the time I post, I've already contributed to the community. It changes how people see your posts—you're not just broadcasting, you're participating."

Engaging Upward: The Hidden Opportunity Inside Your Organization

LinkedIn isn't just a window to the outside world. It's a bridge inside your own company.

For employees, it's one of the most underused ways to connect authentically with senior leaders.

When you engage thoughtfully with their posts—adding insight, not flattery—you signal curiosity, initiative, and alignment with organizational priorities.

According to LinkedIn's internal data, employees who engage with leadership content are 25% more likely to be recognized internally and twice as likely to be considered for stretch assignments or cross-functional projects.

The key is approaching these interactions with the right intent:

Comment to add perspective, not to be seen

Don't just say "Great post!" Add something: a related example, a thoughtful question, a connection to work happening in your part of the organization.

Highlight shared values, not company slogans

Skip the corporate speak. Share how something they mentioned connects to work you're doing or a challenge your team is navigating.

Be consistent, not constant

You don't need to comment on every post. But when you do engage, make it meaningful. Senior leaders remember thoughtful contributors, not frequent flatterers.

In large organizations where physical proximity to leadership is rare, thoughtful LinkedIn engagement can quietly build familiarity and trust—a form of digital visibility that complements your day-to-day work.

One caveat: Never criticize your company publicly on LinkedIn, even constructively. Save that feedback for internal channels. Your LinkedIn presence should reflect professionalism and alignment, even when you're contributing diverse perspectives.

Networking with Key Opinion Leaders

Once your foundation is solid, widen your circle strategically.

Follow thought leaders, practitioners, and voices you want to learn from. But don't just follow—engage.

The slow-burn strategy:

Engage first. Connect later.

When you comment thoughtfully on someone's post, you create visibility in a positive context. Over time, your name becomes familiar—not as a stranger making a cold request, but as someone who contributes to conversations they care about.

This approach has three advantages:

1. **Contextual credibility**

   People see you participating in meaningful discussions, which signals you're worth knowing.

2. **Mutual recognition before connection**

   By the time you send a connection request, they've already seen your name multiple times in contexts that matter to them.

3. Organic door-opening

Sometimes they'll connect with you first, or invite you to participate in something, or mention you in their own content. Opportunities emerge naturally rather than through forced outreach.

When you do connect, lead with authenticity:

"I've really appreciated your insights on Latin American market expansion. Your post last week about localization challenges made me rethink how we approach regional adaptation. I'd value staying connected to continue learning from your perspective."

That's not a template. That's a genuine connection built on demonstrated interest.

Accept invitations generously—with boundaries

If someone's work is relevant to yours, accept the connection. You can always unfollow, mute, or remove them later if needed. The key is openness without naivety.

But if the invitation feels transactional or comes from someone clearly spamming their way to 30,000 connections, you can decline without guilt.

Trust your instincts. Good networkers recognize good networking.

Carolina's approach:

"I engaged with that product manager's posts for six months before we actually connected," she said. "By the time I sent the connection request, he accepted immediately—he already knew who I was. That's so much more powerful than cold messaging someone you've never interacted with."

15 Social Proof and Credibility: Evidence Over Claims

The Woman Who Hid Her Results

Jasmine Ng had been posting on LinkedIn for eight months.

Every evening after work, during her MRT commute from Tanjong Pagar back to her flat in Bedok, she'd scroll through her analytics and feel the familiar frustration.

Jasmine was a Senior Supply Chain Manager at a mid-sized logistics company in Singapore. Fifteen years in the industry. She'd optimized operations for companies moving goods through the Port of Singapore—the world's busiest transshipment hub, where 37 million containers pass through annually.

She knew supply chain management like she knew the MRT map—every connection, every bottleneck, every optimization opportunity.

Her LinkedIn posts were solid—thoughtful takes on supply chain optimization, lessons from her fifteen years in logistics, and frameworks she'd developed through trial and error. Her writing was clear. Her insights were genuine.

But something wasn't working.

Posts would get a handful of likes from colleagues. Maybe a comment or two from friends. Then they'd disappear into the feed, leaving no trace except Jasmine's growing frustration.

She'd watch other professionals—sometimes with less experience—get hundreds of reactions and dozens of comments.

"What am I doing wrong?" she'd ask herself during her evening commute, watching the lights of Singapore blur past the MRT window.

In a city obsessed with efficiency, where optimization is a national pastime, Jasmine had learned to optimize everything.

Everything except her LinkedIn presence.

"You know what your problem is?" her colleague Damien told her one afternoon over kopi at the hawker center near their office. "You're too Singaporean."

Jasmine looked up from her phone. "What does that mean?"

"You work hard, you keep your head down, you let the results speak for themselves. But on LinkedIn, silence means invisible."

Damien had seen Jasmine's work up close. He'd watched her redesign their company's inventory management system from scratch. He knew what she'd achieved. But nobody on LinkedIn did.

"You're not bragging if you're just stating facts," he said. "You saved the company hundreds of thousands of dollars. Why aren't you saying that?"

Jasmine shifted uncomfortably. "It feels like showing off."

"It's not showing off. It's showing proof."

This is the tension many Singaporean professionals face:

In Singapore, you're taught early: work hard, study hard, don't make noise. Humility is valued. Self-promotion is uncomfortable. *Kiasu*—afraid to lose out—yes. But boastful? Never.

But on LinkedIn, in a global professional arena, that cultural modesty becomes career invisibility.

One Tuesday, after another post that barely registered, Damien messaged Jasmine:

"Your content is great, but you're not showing the impact. Nobody knows what you've actually achieved. Add the proof."

Jasmine thought about the inventory management framework she'd been writing about for weeks. She'd shared the theory, the steps, and the philosophy behind lean logistics. But she'd never mentioned the results.

She'd never mentioned that her framework had reduced carrying costs by 23% over six months.

She'd never mentioned that her VP had called it "the most impactful process improvement in five years."

She'd never shared the dashboard showing the before-and-after data.

Why? Because it felt like bragging.

But sitting on the MRT that evening, watching businesspeople around her scrolling their phones, Jasmine had a realization:

If I don't show what I've accomplished, how will anyone know I can help them accomplish the same thing?

She opened LinkedIn and rewrote her post with three elements she'd never used before:

First, a specific metric:

"This approach reduced our carrying costs by 23% over six months."

Second, a quote from her VP:

"Jasmine's system saved us $400K annually while improving our service levels. It's the most impactful process improvement we've made in five years."

Third, a screenshot of the actual dashboard showing the before-and-after data—inventory turnover, carrying costs, order fulfillment rates.

She stared at the post for five minutes before hitting "Share."

This is going to look like I'm showing off. People are going to think I'm bragging.

But she hit Share anyway.

The next morning, she checked her phone during her coffee break.

The post had reached 12,000 people.

Eighty-seven comments. Most from supply chain professionals she'd never met:

- "This is exactly what we're struggling with. Can you share more about your methodology?"

- "23% reduction is impressive. How did you get buy-in from finance?"

- "Would love to hear how you implemented this across multiple warehouses."

Three consulting inquiries landed in her DMs. An invitation to speak at the Singapore Supply Chain Management Association annual conference. Two recruiters from multinational logistics companies.

Same person. Same expertise. Different proof.

What changed wasn't what Jasmine knew. What changed was what she could demonstrate she knew.

This is the invisible line between professionals who sound knowledgeable and professionals who are recognized as authoritative.

The difference is evidence.

Why Claims Without Proof Don't Travel

Every day on LinkedIn, millions of professionals make claims:

"I'm passionate about innovation."

"I drive results."

"I'm a strategic thinker."

"I help companies transform."

These statements might be true. They might even be underselling the person's actual capabilities.

But they share one fatal flaw: they're unverifiable.

In the age of digital professional presence, your words are only as strong as the proof you can show. On LinkedIn, where thousands of voices compete for attention, credibility is what makes one stand out.

For employees, social proof isn't just a nice-to-have. It's the foundation of your personal brand.

This chapter shows you how to anchor your presence not in what you claim, but in what others can verify you've delivered.

The Trust Equation

According to a LinkedIn/Ipsos study on influence, 92% of people trust recommendations from individuals—even strangers—over branded messages.

More striking: when professionals were asked what builds trust in a business context, peer endorsements were rated 3× more influential than competitive pricing.

Let that sink in: proof from peers matters more than product features or cost advantages.

For employees building LinkedIn presence, this means your profile and content must feature not just your opinions or aspirations—but evidence:

✓ Measurable results

✓ Testimonials from people who've worked with you

✓ Examples of work that created impact

✓ Recognition from credible sources

✓ Endorsements from peers in your field

That proof converts visibility into credibility.

And credibility drives opportunity.

Research on personal branding shows that professionals with complete, evidence-rich profiles are 40× more likely to receive opportunities via LinkedIn than those with incomplete profiles.

The mechanism is straightforward: when people can verify your claims, they trust you. When they trust you, they remember you. When they remember you, they think of you when opportunities arise.

What Actually Counts as Social Proof

Not all evidence is created equal. Some forms of social proof carry more weight than others—and the most credible proof often comes from sources you don't control.

Here's the hierarchy, from weakest to strongest:

LEVEL 1: Self-Reported Skills (Weak)

Skills you list on your profile without endorsements. Anyone can claim anything. Low credibility.

LEVEL 2: Endorsed Skills (Moderate)

Skills that others have validated. Better, but can be gamed through reciprocal endorsements between friends.

LEVEL 3: Testimonials from Colleagues (Strong)

Written recommendations from people you've worked with. These carry weight because someone invested time to write about your specific contributions.

LEVEL 4: Quantifiable Results (Stronger)

Metrics, outcomes, measurable impact: "Reduced churn by 15%," "Generated $2M in new revenue," "Cut processing time from 3 weeks to 5 days."

Numbers are harder to dispute than adjectives.

LEVEL 5: Third-Party Recognition (Strongest)

Awards, media mentions, publications, speaking invitations, client testimonials. Proof that comes from outside your direct network carries maximum credibility.

The strongest LinkedIn profiles combine multiple levels. The weakest rely solely on self-reported claims.

What Social Proof Looks Like for Employees:

- ✓ **Recommendations/Testimonials:** Colleagues, managers, or clients describing your impact, contribution, or character in specific terms

- ✓ **Skills and Endorsements:** Validated competencies with endorsements from relevant peers (not just anyone)

- ✓ **Featured Work:** Projects, case studies, presentations, or posts showcasing deliverables, metrics, and lessons learned

- ✓ **Media Mentions or Publications:** External articles, interviews, podcast appearances, or bylined pieces that establish thought leadership

- ✓ **Awards or Recognition:** Industry accolades, internal honors, certifications from credible institutions

- ✓ **Engagement Proof:** Consistent, meaningful comments from respected voices in your field—a form of social validation that happens in public view

LinkedIn's own guidance defines social proof as "the digital signal that others have already trusted or benefited from what you do."

Translation: Don't just tell people you're good at something. Show them that other people think you're good at something.

Jasmine's realization:

"In Singapore, we optimize everything—our MRT system, our port operations, our housing policy. We're obsessed with efficiency backed by data. But when it came to my LinkedIn profile, I was making claims without data. I was violating my own professional principles."

How to Collect Social Proof (Without Being Weird About It)

The hardest part of building social proof isn't knowing it matters. It's overcoming the discomfort of asking for it.

Most professionals—especially employees who aren't naturally self-promotional—feel awkward requesting testimonials or showcasing achievements. It feels like bragging. It feels transactional.

But here's what changed Jasmine's perspective:

"Damien told me: when you ask someone for a recommendation, you're not imposing. You're giving them an opportunity to acknowledge work that mattered to them."

People want to recognize good work. They just need to be asked—specifically and at the right time.

The Right Time to Ask:

1. **After completing a meaningful project**
   Not after every meeting or small task, but after something that created real value. Strike while the impact is fresh in everyone's mind.
   Jasmine's example: After the inventory management project went live and showed six months of sustained results, she asked her VP and the warehouse manager for recommendations.

2. **When someone spontaneously compliments your work**
   If a colleague emails you praise or mentions you positively in a meeting, respond with: "Thank you—would you be willing to write a brief LinkedIn recommendation capturing that?"

3. **Before a career transition**

   Planning to change roles, pursue a promotion, or shift industries? Proactively gather testimonials from people who've seen your best work. You might not have access to them later.

4. **Quarterly, as a professional habit**

   Every ninety days, identify one person whose perspective matters and request a recommendation. Make it routine, not desperate.

The Right Way to Ask:

✖ **Don't say:** "Could you write me a LinkedIn recommendation?"

☑ **Instead:** "I'm building out my LinkedIn profile and would really value your perspective on the inventory management project we worked on together. Would you be willing to write a brief recommendation highlighting how we collaborated and the outcome we achieved?"

This gives them:

- Context (what to focus on)
- A manageable scope (brief)
- A reminder of what you accomplished together

Make it easy:

If they agree but seem busy, offer: "I'm happy to draft something you can edit, to save you time."

Many people will appreciate this—just make sure what you draft is authentic and sounds like their voice.

Jasmine's approach:

"I wrote to my VP: 'I'm updating my LinkedIn profile and would value your perspective on the inventory optimization project. Would you be willing to write a brief recommendation about the impact and how we worked together? I'm happy to draft something you can edit if that's easier.'"

Her VP replied within an hour: "Happy to. Actually, I'll write it myself—you deserve proper recognition for that work."

The recommendation landed two days later. Specific, detailed, with metrics.

Where to Display Your Social Proof

1. Recommendations Section

This is the obvious place, but most people underuse it.

Aim for five to ten high-quality recommendations that span different contexts:

- ✓ Someone you **managed or mentored** (shows leadership)

- ✓ Someone who **managed you** (shows coachability)

- ✓ A **cross-functional partner** (shows collaboration)

- ✓ A **client or external stakeholder** (shows impact)

- ✓ A **peer in your field** (shows respect from equals)

Jasmine's recommendations:

- Her VP (showed strategic impact)

- The warehouse manager (showed operational excellence)

- A finance colleague (showed cross-functional collaboration)

- A client from a major shipping company (showed external validation)

- A supply chain analyst she'd mentored (showed leadership)

2. Featured Section

This is prime real estate—the first thing visitors see after your profile header.

Feature:

- ✓ Your best posts with strong engagement

- ✓ Presentations or reports you've created

✓ Media articles about your work

✓ Case studies or project summaries with metrics

Jasmine's Featured section:

- The inventory optimization post (12K reach, 87 comments)

- A presentation from Singapore Supply Chain Management Association

- A case study: "How We Reduced Carrying Costs by 23% in 6 Months"

- An article from a Singapore logistics industry publication quoting her insights

3. Skills Section (Strategically Curated)

Don't list every skill you've ever touched.

Choose five to ten that align with your value proposition and actively seek endorsements for those specific skills from people whose validation matters.

Jasmine's top skills:

- Supply Chain Optimization (forty-five endorsements)

- Inventory Management (thirty-eight endorsements)

- Logistics Coordination (thirty-two endorsements)

- Process Improvement (twenty-eight endorsements)

- Data Analytics (twenty-five endorsements)

"I removed skills like 'Microsoft Office' and 'Email Marketing' that diluted my positioning," Jasmine said. "Now my skills section tells a clear story: I optimize supply chains using data."

4. Woven into Posts

This is where social proof becomes **dynamic rather than static.**

When you publish content, integrate proof naturally:

Example: "After implementing this framework across three teams, we reduced time-to-market by 30%. My VP called it 'the most impactful process change we've made in five years'. Here's how we did it . . ."

Jasmine's post structure:

Opening: Problem statement (inventory carrying costs too high)

Body: Solution framework (lean inventory principles adapted to Singapore context)

Proof: Results (23% reduction, $400K savings, VP quote)

Value: How others can apply it

Invitation: "What's worked for you in inventory optimization?"

Incorporating Social Proof into Your Content Rhythm

Social proof shouldn't be a one-time profile update. It should be woven into your ongoing LinkedIn presence.

Monthly: Results + Recognition Post

Once a month, share a "here's what we achieved and here's what people said" update.

Keep it brief, results-oriented, and grounded in someone else's words:

Example: "Our team just closed Q2 with 18% growth in customer retention—our best quarter in three years. The client feedback that meant most to me: 'Your team turned a crisis into an opportunity'. That's the work that matters."

Not bragging. Just sharing impact with evidence.

Jasmine's monthly rhythm: First Tuesday of each month, she shares one result from her work with evidence. Doesn't need to be massive—small wins with proof beat big claims without evidence.

Quarterly: Profile Audit

Every ninety days, review and refresh:

✓ Remove outdated skills that no longer align with your positioning

✓ Request one new recommendation from someone you've worked with recently

✓ Update your Featured section with your best recent work

✓ Ensure your profile tells a coherent story backed by evidence

Jasmine's quarterly checklist:

- Review recommendations (any outdated?)

- Add latest project to Featured section

- Request one new recommendation

- Update headline if positioning has evolved

- Check that skills align with current role

Before Key Events: Fresh Testimonials

Planning to attend a major conference? Applying for an internal promotion? Exploring a career pivot?

Gather fresh testimonials beforehand. Position them prominently. Let proof do the heavy lifting while you focus on the opportunity.

Jasmine's preparation for Singapore Supply Chain Week:

Two weeks before speaking at the conference, she:

- Updated her Featured section with recent projects

- Requested a recommendation from a recent client

- Posted about preparing her presentation (with metrics from past work)

- Made sure her profile reflected her expertise

When conference attendees looked her up, they found a profile backed by evidence.

In Every Significant Post: Integrate Proof

Don't just share ideas—share results:

Formula: "After leading this initiative, we achieved [metric]. The feedback from [role/person]: '[quote]'. Here's what worked . . ."

By consistently weaving proof into your narrative, you transform your posts from interesting opinions into credible insights.

Jasmine's formula:

$$\text{Problem} \rightarrow \text{Solution} \rightarrow \text{Results} \rightarrow \text{Proof} \rightarrow \text{Learning} \rightarrow \text{Invitation}$$

Every post follows this structure. Every post includes at least one form of social proof.

Ethics: The Line Between Proof and Performance

Because proof is powerful, it's also vulnerable to manipulation.

Some professionals manufacture credibility: buying fake endorsements, inflating metrics, claiming credit for team outcomes, or selectively showcasing only the wins while hiding every failure.

This creates a short-term appearance of credibility. It also creates long-term reputational risk.

Your LinkedIn presence lives forever. So do screenshots. So do memories.

If your proof doesn't hold up to scrutiny, the damage to your reputation will far outweigh any temporary visibility gains.

Guidelines for Ethical Social Proof:

1. **Don't fabricate outcomes**

   If an initiative is still in progress, frame it honestly: "We're six months into this transformation and early results show 15% improvement. Here's what we're learning . . ."

2. **Don't pay for endorsements**

   LinkedIn will flag suspicious patterns. Your network will sense inauthenticity. The trust you're trying to build will evaporate.

3. **Always get permission before quoting others**

   If someone gave you feedback in private, ask before making it public. Respect confidentiality and context.

   Jasmine's practice: "Before I quoted my VP in my post, I messaged him: 'Would you be comfortable with me sharing your feedback publicly on LinkedIn?' He said yes, and even suggested I use his title for added credibility."

4. **Don't claim credit that isn't yours**

   Be specific about your contribution to team outcomes.

   "I led the analysis that uncovered . . ." or "Our team delivered, and my role was . . ."

   This shows confidence without claiming false ownership.

   Jasmine's language: "Our team reduced carrying costs by 23%. My role was redesigning the inventory framework and leading implementation across three warehouses."

   Clear contribution. Clear team acknowledgment.

5. **Keep proof relevant to your audience**

   Highlighting that you won your company's ping-pong tournament won't build professional credibility (unless you're in sports management).

   Make sure your proof aligns with what your audience actually values.

6. **Be honest about failures alongside successes**

   The most credible professionals don't only showcase wins. They acknowledge what didn't work and what they learned.

   Selective perfection destroys trust faster than honest imperfection.

   Jasmine's vulnerability post: "Three years ago, I tried to implement this same framework. It failed spectacularly. Here are the three mistakes I made—and what I learned that led to success the second time."

   That post got more engagement than her success post. People trust people who admit mistakes.

A LinkedIn article on credibility warns: "Social proof isn't just nice—it's a signal. If the signal is weak or manufactured, the trust evaporates instantly."

Your reputation is built over years and destroyed in moments. Protect it.

Three Types of Proof Posts (Templates You Can Use)

1. The Results Post

"Three months ago, our team set an ambitious goal: reduce customer onboarding time from 14 days to 5. Yesterday we closed our first customer in 4 days. The feedback from our Head of Operations: 'This changes everything for how we scale'. Here's the framework we used . . ."

Why it works: Metric + timeline + third-party validation + educational value

Jasmine's version: "Six months ago, our carrying costs were 18% above industry benchmark. Last week, we hit 23% below benchmark—saving $400K annually. The feedback from our VP: 'This is the most impactful process improvement we've made in five years'. Here's the framework . . ."

2. The Recognition Post

"Grateful to be recognized as a LinkedIn Top Voice in Supply Chain Management. What made this meaningful: it's based on how the community engages with the ideas I share, not just how much I post. That reinforces what I believe—substance over frequency."

Why it works: External validation + humble framing + alignment with values

Jasmine's version: "Honored to speak at Singapore Supply Chain Week next month. What makes this meaningful: two years ago, I attended as an attendee, taking notes. Now I'm sharing what we've learned. That's the power of documenting your work and sharing what you learn."

3. The Testimonial-Driven Post

"Last week, a former colleague reached out: 'James, I still use that decision framework you taught me five years ago. It's saved me countless hours and countless mistakes'. This is why I share what I learn—because frameworks travel, and good ideas compound."

Why it works: Unprompted testimonial + long-term impact + service mindset

Jasmine's version: "Yesterday, a warehouse manager I trained three years ago messaged me: 'Jasmine, we just hit 99.2% order accuracy using your checklist. Best quarter we've ever had'. This is why I document what works—because good systems outlive projects."

VI Conversion—From Visibility to Opportunity

You've built visibility. You've earned trust. Now comes the moment that separates content creators from career advancers: conversion. This section explores how to translate your LinkedIn presence into tangible outcomes—promotions, collaborations, speaking invitations, and opportunities that wouldn't exist without your digital footprint. Because visibility without outcomes is just noise.

16 From Visibility to Opportunity: Turning LinkedIn Presence into Career Outcomes

The Viral Moment That Changed Nothing

There's a man named David Chen who works as a senior data scientist at a mid-sized fintech company in Silicon Valley.

In January 2023, sitting at a coffee shop in Mountain View—one of those places where half the customers have startup pitch decks open on their laptops and the other half are debugging code—one of his LinkedIn posts exploded.

David had been in the Valley for six years. Long enough to know that everyone here is chasing the next big thing. Long enough to feel the pressure of being surrounded by people who seem more successful, more visible, more everything.

It was a simple visualization showing how AI models fail in unexpected ways—he'd used stick figures and hand-drawn charts to explain complex bias issues. The kind of thing he'd sketch on a whiteboard when explaining algorithms to non-technical colleagues.

The post hit a nerve with technologists, researchers, and people who'd never thought about algorithmic fairness before.

Forty-eight hours later: 90,000 views, 1,200 likes, and 230 comments.

Tech journalists were messaging him. Conference organizers wanted him to speak. His follower count jumped from 800 to 4,200 overnight.

David felt like he'd finally broken through.

"In Silicon Valley, everyone talks about going viral," he told me over video call last month. "I'd been watching other data scientists—people with less experience than me—get invited to conferences, quoted in articles, recognized at meetups. And I kept thinking: when is it going to be my turn?"

Then it happened. And for forty-eight hours, David felt like he'd made it.

But then something strange happened: nothing.

The invitations dried up after the initial rush. The new followers never engaged with his next posts. Three months later, he was back to his usual thirty views and five likes per post—except now, with 4,000 followers instead of 800, which somehow felt worse.

The viral moment came and went like a summer storm. It changed the weather for forty-eight hours, but it didn't change the climate.

What happened?

David had visibility without positioning. When people asked "Who is this person and what do they stand for?" there was no clear answer. His profile said "Data Scientist" but didn't explain what kind of problems he solved or who he helped. His previous posts were scattered—leadership advice one day, weekend photos the next, an occasional data tutorial.

The viral post was a doorway, but there was no house behind it.

When opportunity knocked, David had nothing ready to offer: no clear expertise, no consistent message, no way to convert attention into relationship.

One year later, David still has 4,200 followers. His posts still average thirty views. The viral moment became just that—a moment, not a movement.

"I watched the follower count go up and thought: finally, I'm being seen," David said. "But I wasn't prepared for what comes after being seen. I didn't know what I wanted people to see me as."

The Viral Moment That Changed Everything

Now consider Priya Sharma.

She works in talent development at a global consulting firm in Mumbai, India. Her office is in BKC—Bandra Kurla Complex, Mumbai's business district where glass towers house consulting firms, banks, and multinational headquarters.

Every morning, Priya takes the Western Line local train from Andheri to BKC. The commute gives her time to scroll LinkedIn, read industry news, and think about the talent challenges her firm faces.

In March 2023, stuck in Mumbai traffic in an Uber after a particularly long day, she posted about a hiring mistake she'd made.

She'd accidentally rejected a candidate who turned out to be perfect for the role. Not because of his qualifications—those were strong. But because his résumé didn't fit the traditional consulting profile: IIT degree, Big 4 experience, impeccable English.

He'd gone to a regional engineering college. Worked at a mid-sized Indian company. His English was confident but accented.

Priya almost passed. Then she caught herself: *Am I hiring for credentials or for capability?*

She called him back. Apologized for the initial rejection. Hired him. Six months later, he was one of the highest-performing analysts on her team.

She posted about this mistake—the awkward conversation when she had to call him back, the assumptions she'd made, what she'd learned about hiring for potential instead of pedigree.

The post was vulnerable, funny, and deeply relatable. It went viral in HR and consulting circles across India and beyond: sixty-five thousand views, nine hundred likes, and one hundred and fifty comments from talent professionals sharing their own stories.

But unlike David, Priya was ready.

Her profile clearly stated her positioning: "I help companies hire for potential, not just pedigree."

Her featured section showcased articles she'd written about inclusive hiring practices in the Indian market—how to recognize talent from non-traditional backgrounds, how to look beyond IIT/IIM credentials, how to build diverse teams in a credential-obsessed culture.

Her content history was consistent—every post explored talent, bias, or how to recognize potential others miss.

When recruiters and conference organizers reached out, she had something substantial to offer: a clear point of view, a track record of thinking deeply about hiring, and a body of work that proved she wasn't a one-hit wonder.

Six months after the viral post, Priya had:

- ✓ Spoken at three major HR conferences (including People Matters TechHR in Gurgaon)
- ✓ Been quoted in two business publications (*Economic Times* and *Business Standard*)
- ✓ Launched a monthly LinkedIn newsletter on hiring practices in India (now 8,000 subscribers)
- ✓ Been promoted to Director of Talent Strategy

Her viral moment became a launchpad because she had a platform to launch from.

Same visibility. Different outcome. The difference? Preparation.

"In Mumbai, we're taught that credentials are everything," Priya told me. "IIT, IIM, Big 4. That's the golden path. But I'd been questioning that for years. When my post went viral, it wasn't luck. It was validation that other people were questioning it too. And I was ready to lead that conversation."

The Visibility Paradox

This is what we might call the visibility paradox: building a LinkedIn presence is only the first step. The real question is what you do with that presence.

Visibility creates awareness. Credibility creates outcomes.

Understanding the difference between the two is what separates professionals who post from professionals who progress.

David and Priya both experienced viral moments. Both received attention, inquiries, and follower spikes. But only one converted that visibility into tangible career outcomes. Not because Priya was luckier or more talented, but because she understood something David didn't:

Visibility without strategy is just noise.

Think of it like this: imagine you're at a networking event and someone stands on a table and shouts "I'M HERE!" Everyone turns to look. You have their attention—for about ten seconds. Then they turn back to their conversations.

Now imagine someone else who's been circulating the room for an hour, having meaningful conversations, sharing insights, helping people connect. When that person stands up to share an idea, people lean in. They're already invested. They already trust.

That's the difference between viral moments and sustained influence.

David's reflection:

"In Silicon Valley, everyone's obsessed with the 'big break' moment. Your startup gets funded. Your post goes viral. You get quoted in TechCrunch. But nobody talks about what you do after the break. I had my moment, and I had no idea what to do with it."

Priya's reflection:

"I'd been posting consistently about talent and hiring for 18 months before my post went viral. When it happened, I didn't see it as a lucky break. I saw it as amplification of something I'd already been building. That's why I was ready."

The Trust Equation

In 2024, researchers at LinkedIn partnered with Ipsos to study what makes someone influential on professional platforms. They surveyed thousands of professionals across industries and asked a simple question:

When you're evaluating whether someone is a thought leader in their field, what matters most?

The results were striking: 93% of respondents agreed that trust and credibility were more important than reach.

Not slightly more important. Significantly more important.

You could have 100,000 followers and minimal influence, or 5,000 followers and substantial impact. The difference isn't the size of your audience. It's the quality of your reputation.

This finding echoes research published in the *Journal of Business and Psychology*, where scholars studying personal branding behavior discovered **a** correlation coefficient of 0.48 between personal branding and perceived employability. That's a moderately strong relationship in social science terms.

But here's what's interesting: the correlation wasn't with how much someone posted, or how many followers they had, or how often content went viral.

The correlation was with how posts signaled value, competence, and trustworthiness over time.

David's viral post signaled cleverness. Priya's viral post signaled expertise backed by consistent positioning.

One was a spark. The other was evidence of a fire already burning.

This is the trust equation:

Visibility opens doors. Credibility keeps them open.

The Three-Stage Progression

Think of LinkedIn presence as three interconnected stages, each building on the last:

Stage 1: Visibility

You post, you comment, you show up. People start recognizing your name. They know you exist.

This is necessary but insufficient. It's like being on the guest list at a networking event—you're in the room, but that doesn't mean anyone wants to talk to you yet.

David had visibility. So did Priya. So does anyone who posts consistently.

Stage 2: Credibility

This is where transformation happens.

You begin sharing content that solves problems, adds insight, or teaches something new. Your posts shift from self-expression to service. You're no longer just visible—you're valuable.

People don't just recognize your name; they associate it with specific expertise, particular insights, or useful frameworks.

Priya reached this stage. David didn't. The difference showed up when opportunity came calling.

Stage 3: Opportunity

Here, visibility and credibility compound into outcomes.

You receive messages about roles, projects, or collaborations. Senior leaders remember your name in meetings. Clients invite you to conversations. The system you've built starts working for you, often in ways you didn't anticipate.

This progression mirrors what researchers at Edelman discovered in their Trust Barometer studies: competence and ethics together drive 88% of perceived trust in professional interactions.

Not charisma. Not visibility. Competence and ethics.

The ability to deliver value, combined with the integrity to deliver it honestly.

David's journey:

"I realized I was stuck at Stage 1. I was visible to 4,200 people, but credible to none of them. I'd never articulated what I stood for, what problems I solved, or why anyone should care about my perspective."

Priya's journey:

"I spent 18 months building credibility before my viral moment. Every post was about hiring, talent, or leadership. When opportunity came, people knew exactly what I offered."

The Career Accelerator

Here's a statistic that should make every professional pay attention:

77% of recruiters use LinkedIn as their primary tool to identify and vet candidates.

Not job boards. Not referrals. LinkedIn.

And professionals with complete, well-optimized profiles receive 40× more opportunities than those without.

Let that sink in. Forty times.

This isn't about gaming the system. It's about understanding what LinkedIn has become: a career accelerator disguised as a social platform.

Your digital presence has become part of your résumé. When you post insights from a project, share learning takeaways, or engage thoughtfully with your firm's leaders, you're performing what economists call signaling.

You're sending visible, searchable signals about:

✓ How you think

✓ What you value

✓ How you contribute

✓ What problems you solve

Consider what happens when you post about solving a client challenge. You're not just sharing a story—you're signaling problem-solving ability.

When you reflect on leadership lessons, you're signaling self-awareness and strategic thinking.

When you create a carousel simplifying complex data, you're signaling communication skills and analytical depth.

These are what behavioral scientists call social signals. And research on signaling theory in career development shows that employees who share evidence of expertise online are more likely to be perceived as competent and promotable—especially when supported by consistent engagement and peer endorsement.

In other words: every post is a career signal.

The question is whether those signals are adding up to a coherent narrative about who you are and what you can do.

David's signals were scattered. Priya's signals were consistent and clear.

When opportunity evaluated them, it was obvious who had something to offer.

David's realization (twelve months later):

"I was sending random signals. One day I'm posting about AI ethics. Next day, a hiking photo. Then leadership advice. Then a meme. My profile didn't tell a story. It was just . . . noise."

Priya's strategy:

"Every post I wrote, I asked myself: does this reinforce my positioning as someone who understands talent and hiring in the Indian market? If the answer was no, I didn't post it."

The Hidden Multiplier: Internal Visibility

Here's something that surprises many people: one of the most underrated benefits of LinkedIn activity is internal visibility. Not external. Internal.

When your leaders, colleagues, and HR department see your insights in their feed, something subtle but powerful happens. You move from being a name on an email thread to a professional voice associated with clarity and leadership.

You become, in organizational psychology terms, "cognitively available."

When opportunities arise—a stretch project, a cross-functional initiative, a high-visibility assignment—your name surfaces more readily because you've been showing up consistently in people's consciousness.

A LinkedIn internal survey discovered that employees who actively engage with company or leadership content are 25% more likely to be recognized by management. But here's the striking part: they're twice as likely to be offered stretch assignments or cross-functional opportunities.

Not because they're better at their jobs, necessarily, but because they're more visible in the right contexts.

The logic is elegantly simple: when you consistently show up with insights that reflect your company's purpose or values, you become visible for the right reasons. You're not just doing your job—you're demonstrating that you understand the bigger picture.

This creates what we might call the echo effect.

Your digital reputation echoes into your workplace reputation. The thoughtful comment you leave on your CEO's post about innovation gets noticed. The reflection you share about a cross-functional project gets circulated. The insight you offer about industry trends gets referenced in meetings you're not even in.

Priya's internal visibility:

After her viral post, she didn't chase another viral moment. Instead, she started posting more deliberately about the specific challenges her firm faced in the Indian market.

She wrote about what she was learning from projects, not just what she'd accomplished. She engaged thoughtfully with posts from senior leaders in her organization—adding perspective about the Indian talent market, not flattery.

Six months later, she was invited to present at an internal strategy meeting. The invitation came from a senior partner who'd been following her posts.

"I wanted someone who understood both the technical details of recruiting and the strategic implications for our India practice," he told her later. "Your LinkedIn presence told me you were that person."

That's internal visibility converting to internal opportunity.

David's missed opportunity:

"Nobody at my company followed me on LinkedIn. I'd never engaged with company posts. Never commented on our CEO's updates. I was building external visibility while being invisible internally. That was backward."

The Conversion Framework

Once you've built consistent visibility and credibility, the next stage is actively converting that into opportunity. Not through aggressive self-promotion, but through strategic documentation and intelligent follow-through.

1. Document Outcomes

Keep a record of posts that led to tangible actions:

- ✓ Messages from recruiters
- ✓ Project invitations
- ✓ Client leads
- ✓ Positive feedback from leadership
- ✓ Speaking opportunities
- ✓ Media inquiries

These become data points not just for analytics, but for your next performance review. They're evidence of impact that extends beyond your job description.

Priya's practice:

Maintained a simple spreadsheet tracking which posts generated which opportunities. When promotion time came, she had quantifiable evidence that her thought leadership was creating value for the organization.

Columns in her spreadsheet:

- Post topic
- Date published
- Engagement metrics
- Opportunities generated
- Outcome

David's mistake:

Didn't track anything. When opportunities faded, he had no way to understand what worked or how to recreate it.

2. Track Who's Engaging

Are they senior colleagues? Decision-makers? Potential clients? Peers whose respect you value?

Engagement from the right audience matters infinitely more than sheer numbers.

A post that generates five thoughtful comments from influential people in your field is more valuable than a post that generates a hundred likes from random connections.

Priya's tracking:

> "I noticed that senior partners in my firm were liking and commenting on my posts about inclusive hiring. That told me I was building credibility with the people who mattered for my career."

3. Respond Promptly to Professional Dialogue

Researchers studying online professional behavior have found that response speed is one of the strongest signals of credibility.

When someone reaches out and you respond within hours (not days), you're communicating that you take relationships seriously.

Priya's practice:

Responded to every meaningful inquiry within twenty-four hours. Many of her biggest opportunities came from second or third exchanges—conversations that would never have happened if she'd been slow to respond.

4. Share Impact Stories Strategically

When a project delivers measurable results, document it with insights:

✘ **Outcome only:** "We improved efficiency by 30%."

☑ **Thought leadership:** "We improved efficiency by 30%—here's what worked, what didn't, and what we learned that might help you."

The difference is subtle but profound. One is self-promotion. The other is contribution.

Priya's formula:

Result + Method + Learning + Invitation

"We increased offer acceptance rates by 40% among candidates from non-traditional backgrounds. Here's how we changed our interview process. Here's what surprised us. What's worked for you in inclusive hiring?"

5. Build Relationships, Not Just Connections

The best opportunities don't come from your 5,000 connections. They come from the fifty people who actually know what you stand for.

Focus on depth over breadth. Nurture meaningful professional relationships. Follow up. Stay in touch. Add value without asking for anything.

Priya's network strategy:

2,400 connections. But she'd built genuine relationships with about 100 people who respected her work and would advocate for her.

David's network reality:

4,200 connections. But David had followers who barely remembered his name.

When opportunity requires a recommendation or introduction, relationships matter. Connections don't.

The Halo Effect

In 2024, Harvard Business Review Analytic Services published a study quantifying something many professionals suspected but couldn't prove:

Employees who maintain an active, credible presence online are perceived as 21% more innovative and 27% more likely to be seen as future leaders by both peers and supervisors.

Think about what that means.

Your online presence doesn't just affect how external people perceive you. It affects how your own colleagues and bosses perceive you.

The act of consistently sharing insights, engaging thoughtfully, and contributing value creates a halo effect that extends into how people evaluate your everyday work.

This is what we might call the influence compound effect.

Every post that adds value, every comment that clarifies a thought, every connection that broadens perspective—it all quietly compounds over time. You don't see it happening day to day. But over months and years, it accumulates into something substantial.

Until one day it shows up in your annual review. Or in a conversation about who should lead the next major initiative. Or in a recruiter's email about an opportunity you didn't apply for.

Your online credibility becomes an invisible currency, exchanged for trust, visibility, and leadership potential.

Priya's promotion:

Didn't happen because of her viral post. It happened because she'd spent eighteen months demonstrating consistent expertise, thoughtful leadership, and genuine desire to help others solve problems. The viral post was just amplification of something already true.

David's viral post:

Was an anomaly. There was nothing to amplify.

The Vanity Trap

There's a mistake that's easy to make and costly to commit: confusing reach with relevance.

David's viral post had reach. Ninety thousand views is impressive. But those 90,000 people weren't decision-makers in his career. They weren't his bosses, his potential clients, or the people who could offer him opportunities. They were, by and large, strangers who appreciated a clever visualization and moved on.

This is the vanity trap. The pursuit of metrics that feel good but mean little. The chase for viral moments that generate brief dopamine spikes but no lasting impact.

A LinkedIn study on thought leadership found that 64% of decision-makers said thought leadership content was a more trustworthy basis for assessing expertise than marketing materials.

Notice what they didn't say. They didn't say the content with the most likes, or the most shares, or the most viral potential. They said thought leadership content. Substance over sensation.

The goal isn't to become famous. It's to become trusted and valuable within your domain.

The algorithm changes. Human trust doesn't.

Build for trust, not for trends.

17 Measurement and Growth: Tracking Results and Evolving Your Presence

The Problem with Flying Blind

For six months, Rina Santoso posted on LinkedIn every Tuesday and Thursday.

Same routine: During her evening commute home—usually spent stuck in Jakarta's legendary traffic, watching the sun set over the skyline from her Transjakarta bus or scrolling on her phone in a Grab—she'd write something thoughtful about supply chain management, hit publish, and hope for the best.

Rina was a Senior Supply Chain Manager at a mid-sized manufacturing company in South Jakarta. Eight years in the industry, most of it spent optimizing operations in Indonesia's complex logistics environment.

She knew the challenges intimately: navigating traffic that could turn a ten-kilometer delivery into a three-hour ordeal, managing shipments across thousands of Indonesian islands, and dealing with infrastructure gaps that would never appear in a Harvard Business Review case study.

Her work was valuable. She'd saved her company millions of rupiah by redesigning distribution networks. She'd trained dozens of logistics coordinators. She understood supply chain complexity in ways most textbooks didn't cover.

But on LinkedIn, her voice seemed to disappear into the void.

Some posts got thirty likes. Others got three. She couldn't figure out the pattern.

Her follower count crept upward—from 450 to 680 over six months. Progress, technically. But slow. Inconsistent. Frustrating.

She'd look at other supply chain professionals—people based in Singapore, people in the United States, people who'd started posting after her—and watch them gain hundreds of engaged followers while her numbers barely moved.

"Maybe I'm just not good at this," she'd think during the two-hour commute from her office in Sudirman to her apartment in South Jakarta, closing LinkedIn for the third time that day.

"Maybe LinkedIn is for people who speak perfect English. Maybe it's for people in Singapore or San Francisco, not Jakarta."

Then one Thursday afternoon, sitting in her kitchen after a particularly disappointing post (four likes, zero comments), the AC humming against Jakarta's afternoon heat, Rina did something she'd been avoiding for months:

She actually looked at her analytics.

She'd been scared to look. Scared the numbers would confirm what she feared—that her content wasn't good enough, that she was wasting her time, and that maybe LinkedIn just wasn't for her.

"I kept thinking: what if the data proves I'm terrible at this?" she told me over video call last month. "What if all those hours I spent writing posts in English— checking every sentence twice, making sure the grammar was right—what if it was all for nothing?"

But sitting there in her kitchen, laptop open on the table, she finally clicked into her analytics dashboard.

What she discovered changed everything.

Her Tuesday posts consistently got 3x more engagement than her Thursday posts.

Her carousels outperformed her text-only posts by 400%.

Posts about real problems she'd solved—like reducing warehouse turnaround time by 35% or optimizing routes through Jakarta traffic—generated meaningful comments and saves.

Posts about generic industry trends got polite likes and nothing more.

The data had been screaming at her for months. She'd just never listened.

Rina stared at the screen, scrolling through six months of numbers. The pattern was so clear, so obvious, she couldn't believe she'd missed it.

"I felt stupid and relieved at the same time," she said. "Stupid because the answers were right there all along. Relieved because it meant I wasn't bad at LinkedIn—I was just posting the wrong things at the wrong times."

Rina made three changes based on what the numbers told her:

1. **Stopped posting on Thursdays** (when her audience was least active)

2. **Shifted to carousels** for framework-based content (supply chain processes, optimization frameworks, problem-solving methods)

3. **Focused exclusively on problem-solution stories** from her actual work in Indonesia

Three months later:

- Tuesday posts averaging 150+ engagements

- Comment threads with genuine dialogue from supply chain professionals across Southeast Asia

- Two speaking invitations (including Indonesia Supply Chain Forum)

- A promotion conversation with her boss that explicitly mentioned her "thought leadership presence"

What changed wasn't her content quality or her expertise.

What changed was that she started measuring what actually worked—and doing more of that.

This is the invisible wall most LinkedIn users hit: they post, they hope, they wonder why growth feels random.

The professionals who break through that wall? They measure. They learn. They iterate.

This chapter shows you how.

Why Most People Avoid Their Analytics (And Why That's Costly)

Let's be honest: most professionals avoid looking at their LinkedIn analytics for the same reason people avoid stepping on a scale or checking their bank balance.

They're afraid of what they'll find.

"What if my posts aren't as good as I thought?"

"What if I'm wasting my time?"

"What if the data confirms I'm failing?"

But here's the truth: not knowing is more expensive than knowing.

When you don't measure, you repeat mistakes. You waste effort on content that doesn't resonate. You miss opportunities to double down on what works. You build momentum in the wrong direction, or worse—you build no momentum at all.

Data isn't judgment. Data is information. And information is what separates random posting from strategic growth.

In the early days of LinkedIn, posting frequently might have been enough. But as the platform matures, volume alone isn't the driver. Insight, relevance, and consistency are.

According to industry benchmark studies:

- **Median engagement rate on LinkedIn:** 4.73% (by impressions)
- **Average engagement rate Q1 2025:** 3.4% across all sectors
- **Smaller accounts (<5K followers):** ~6% engagement rate
- **Large accounts (>100K followers):** ~3% engagement rate

Translation: If you're a smaller account, your engagement rate should actually be higher than mega-influencers. If it's not, something's off—and the analytics will tell you what.

Without measurement, you're flying blind. With measurement, you can see where you're going and adjust course before you hit the ground.

The Metrics That Actually Matter (And the Ones That Don't)

Not all LinkedIn metrics are created equal. Some signal real impact. Others are just vanity numbers that make you feel good for ten seconds but mean nothing for your career.

Here's how to tell the difference:

Vanity Metrics (Feel Good, Mean Little)

✖ **Total Impressions**
"My post got 10,000 views!"
But who saw it? Did they care? Did they remember your name five minutes later?
Impressions without engagement are just digital noise.

✖ **Follower Count**
"I have 5,000 followers!"
But how many actually see your posts? How many would recognize your name at a conference?
Followers who don't engage are digital ghosts.

✖ **Likes**
"I got 200 likes!"
But did anyone save your post? Share it? Comment meaningfully? Message you about it?
Likes are cheap. Anyone can double-tap while scrolling.

Impact Metrics (Actually Predict Outcomes)

☑ **Engagement Rate**
(Reactions + Comments + Shares) ÷ Impressions
This tells you what percentage of people who saw your content actually cared enough to interact.
Target: 4–6% for accounts under 5K followers, 3–5% for larger accounts.

☑ **Comments (Quality, Not Quantity)**

Not just count—**depth**. Are people sharing experiences? Asking follow-up questions? Tagging colleagues?

One meaningful three-sentence comment beats twenty emoji reactions.

☑ **Shares and Saves**

These signal that your content was valuable enough to bookmark or amplify. **Saves especially matter**—LinkedIn's algorithm heavily weights this as a quality signal.

☑ **Profile Views After Posting**

Did your post make people curious enough to click through to your profile? This is early-stage conversion: **awareness → interest**.

☑ **Connection Requests from Relevant People**

Are you attracting peers, senior leaders, or people in your target industry? Or just random salespeople and cryptocurrency schemes?

☑ **Direct Messages About Opportunities**

Speaking invitations, collaboration requests, job inquiries, client leads. This is late-stage conversion: **interest → opportunity**.

☑ **Search Appearances and Who's Viewing Your Profile**

Are the right people finding you? If you're trying to build credibility in supply chain but getting views from wedding photographers, your positioning needs work.

Rina's discovery:

Her Tuesday posts had **6.2% engagement rate** versus Thursday's **1.8%**.

That wasn't random. That was data telling her where her audience was paying attention.

Tuesday 8 AM Jakarta time (GMT + 7):

- Indonesia professionals starting workday
- Singapore/Malaysia professionals at their desks
- Australia winding down afternoon
- US West Coast evening (some checking before bed)

Thursday 3 PM Jakarta time:

- Indonesia professionals leaving work early

- Singapore wrapping up

- Everyone else already disconnected

Once she knew, she could act.

VII Sustainability— Ethics, Mindset, and Longevity

You've built a presence. You're converting visibility into opportunity. But the final test isn't whether you can start—it's whether you can sustain. This section explores the ethical boundaries that protect your reputation, the mindset shifts that prevent burnout, and the long-term strategies that transform LinkedIn from a project into a practice. Because building something that lasts requires more than strategy. It requires wisdom.

18 Ethics and Professional Boundaries: Navigating LinkedIn with Integrity

The Post That Cost Everything

On a Tuesday morning in 2023, Judy Miller posted a photo on LinkedIn.

She was sitting at her desk in Midtown Atlanta—one of those open-plan offices in Tech Square where you can hear three different Zoom calls happening simultaneously and someone's always brewing coffee that smells better than it tastes.

Judy had been a product manager at a mid-sized SaaS company for three years, consistently delivering results but rarely getting recognition. While her colleagues in San Francisco and New York seemed to effortlessly build LinkedIn followings, Judy felt invisible in Atlanta's quieter tech scene.

So when her team finally cracked a strategy problem they'd been wrestling with for months, she felt proud. Excited. Visible.

The photo was innocent enough: a whiteboard from their breakthrough session, covered in sticky notes and diagrams. The caption read: "Exciting new direction for Q4—can't wait to share more soon! 🚀"

Within an hour, sitting in the third-floor conference room for her next meeting, watching the notifications roll in, Judy felt a rush she hadn't experienced in months.

140 likes. Twelve comments. People from her network—former colleagues, Atlanta tech meetup connections, product managers she'd met at conferences—all congratulating her, asking questions, cheering her on.

In Atlanta's growing tech scene, where everyone seemed to be one LinkedIn post away from their next opportunity, Judy finally felt like she was being seen.

Then her manager Slacked her: "Can you come to my office?"

Judy walked down the hall, still riding the high from the engagement. Maybe he'd seen the post. Maybe he wanted to congratulate her too.

He closed the door behind her.

"Judy, we need to talk about your LinkedIn post."

One of those twelve comments had come from a competitor—someone Judy had connected with months earlier at an Atlanta Tech Village networking event. That person had zoomed in on the whiteboard, spotted three client names clearly visible in the photo, along with a Q4 launch timeline and what looked like a pricing strategy.

They'd screenshot the image. Shared it with their product team. Immediately adjusted their own roadmap.

Six weeks later, Judy's company lost a major deal to that competitor.

The investigation traced the leak back to one LinkedIn post. One photo. One moment of enthusiasm that seemed completely harmless.

Judy wasn't fired—but the promotion conversation that had been scheduled for that quarter was quietly postponed. Indefinitely.

That night, Judy sat in her car in the parking garage of her Midtown office for twenty minutes before driving home, watching the sun set through the concrete pillars, replaying the meeting over and over.

She opened LinkedIn on her phone. The post was still there. 140 likes. Twelve comments. All the validation she'd craved, now poisoned by what it had cost.

She deleted the post. But screenshots live forever.

"I didn't think anyone would actually look that closely," she told her partner later that evening, sitting at their kitchen table in their Virginia-Highland apartment. "It was just a whiteboard. I was just proud of our work."

But LinkedIn isn't just a whiteboard. It's a billboard.

Visible to everyone, permanent, searchable, and screenshot-able.

Every post, every comment, every reaction carries two signatures: your name and your employer's reputation.

This chapter is about understanding that dual responsibility—and learning to navigate it without sacrificing authenticity, dampening your voice, or living in fear of saying the wrong thing.

Because the goal isn't to silence you. The goal is to help you speak with both confidence and wisdom.

So what happened to Judy doesn't happen to you.

Why Ethics Isn't Just About Not Getting Fired

Most people think about LinkedIn ethics only when they're worried about getting in trouble.

"Can I post this without HR getting mad?"

"Will this violate my NDA?"

"Am I allowed to say this?"

These are important questions. But they're not the only questions—or even the most important ones.

Here's what most professionals miss: ethics isn't just about avoiding punishment. It's about building credibility.

According to the 2024 Edelman Trust Barometer, 61% of people trust "someone like themselves" more than official company statements. Your voice, as an employee, carries more weight than your CEO's press release.

But that influence comes with responsibility. When you post on LinkedIn, you're not just representing yourself. You're representing:

✓ Your team

✓ Your company

✓ Your industry

✓ Your profession

And in an era where 90% of employers review social media profiles before making hiring or promotion decisions (CareerBuilder, 2023), and 70% of professionals say a colleague's online behavior affects their perception of that person at work (PwC Global Workforce Survey, 2024), your digital presence isn't separate from your professional reputation.

It is your professional reputation.

Think of it this way: your LinkedIn profile is like wearing your company's logo on your shirt. Even when you're off the clock, people associate what you say with where you work.

That's not a limitation. It's leverage—if you use it wisely.

Judy's realization:

"I worked so hard to be visible. To get noticed. To have people see my work. But I didn't think about who was watching or what they could see. In Atlanta's tech scene, where everyone knows everyone, word travels fast. I should have known better."

The Employee Paradox: Your Voice Matters More (Which Makes Boundaries Matter More)

Here's the paradox every employee faces:

Your voice has more impact than your company's official messaging.

Research confirms this: brand messages shared by employees achieve 561% more reach and 8× more engagement than the same messages shared by official company pages (LinkedIn Marketing Solutions, 2024).

When you post something, people lean in. When your marketing department posts the same thing, people scroll past.

This is a superpower. But like any superpower, it requires responsibility.

The problem? 32% of employees say they're unsure where their employer's brand ends and their own begins (Hootsuite Social Trends Report, 2025).

The result: mixed messages, confused identity, and sometimes—catastrophic mistakes.

The data is sobering:

- 42% of employers report at least one reputational or compliance incident in the past year linked to employees' online behavior (Deloitte Ethics & Compliance Report, 2024)
- 25% of HR professionals have disciplined an employee for social media misconduct—most commonly for breaching confidentiality or misrepresenting company values (CIPD Survey, 2023)

Let that sink in: one in four HR professionals has had to address employee social media issues.

These aren't malicious actors. These are well-intentioned professionals who didn't understand where the line was—or didn't think about it until it was too late.

Judy, from our opening story, wasn't trying to leak competitive intelligence. She was just excited about her work.

But intent doesn't matter to a whiteboard visible in a LinkedIn photo.

The Venn Diagram: Finding Your Authentic Overlap

So how do you balance personal authenticity with professional responsibility?

Think of your LinkedIn presence as a Venn diagram:

CIRCLE 1: Your Personal Brand

Your unique expertise, voice, perspectives, stories, values—what makes you distinctively you.

CIRCLE 2: Your Company's Brand

Your organization's mission, values, culture, strategic direction—what your employer stands for.

The Overlap: Your Sweet Spot

Where your authentic self-aligns with organizational values. This is where you can speak freely, powerfully, and safely.

The mistake most people make: they think these circles are in opposition.

"If I'm authentic, I'll violate company boundaries."

"If I follow company rules, I'll sound like a corporate robot."

False choice.

The truth: the strongest employee voices are those that express personal perspective in service of shared values.

Example of the overlap:

✘ **Outside the overlap:**

"My company's new product is going to crush the competition. Here are the three features that make it unstoppable."
Problem: Makes unapproved product claims, sounds like marketing copy, creates legal risk

☑ **Inside the overlap:**

"I've spent the last six months working on something I'm really proud of— technology that helps people do [specific task] more efficiently. The problem-solving process taught me three lessons about listening to users . . ."
Solution: Personal perspective, shared values, no proprietary details

See the difference?

One is corporate cheerleading that creates risk. The other is authentic contribution that creates value.

The guiding question before you post:

"Does this represent how I want to be seen—and how my company should be seen?"

If the answer is yes to both, you're in the overlap. Post with confidence.

If the answer is no to either, reconsider.

Judy's lesson:

"I was so focused on 'Does this make me look good?' that I never asked 'Does this put my company at risk?' I thought those were the same question. They're not."

The Hidden Cost of Well-Intentioned Oversharing

Here's what most people don't realize: the biggest reputational risks don't come from malice. They come from enthusiasm.

A Deloitte Risk Advisory study (2023) found that 68% of data-leak incidents involving employees began with non-malicious intent—often through public posts, screenshots, or comments that exposed internal details.

The IBM Cost of Insider Threats Report (2024) estimated that unintentional data disclosure costs companies an average of $4.9 million per incident, up 11% from the year before.

$4.9 million. From someone who just wanted to share their excitement.

Common scenarios where good intentions create problems:

SCENARIO 1: The Proud Team Photo

You post a photo of your team celebrating a project milestone. Visible in the background: a monitor displaying client names, revenue figures, or unreleased product features.

SCENARIO 2: The Behind-the-Scenes Story

You share a "day in the life" post that mentions you're working with a specific client—who hasn't publicly announced the partnership yet.

SCENARIO 3: The Helpful Resource

You screenshot an internal framework or process document to share with your network—accidentally including proprietary methodologies or confidential data.

SCENARIO 4: The Casual Comment

You comment on someone's post about industry trends, casually mentioning what your company is planning for next quarter—information that's not yet public.

None of these feel malicious. All of them create risk.

The Protection Framework:

Before sharing anything about your work, ask:

1. **Is this information already public?**

   If it's not in a press release, on your company website, or approved for external sharing—don't post it.

2. **Would a competitor find this useful?**

   If yes, don't post it. Even seemingly innocuous details (client names, project timelines, and strategic priorities) are competitive intelligence.

3. **Could this photo/screenshot reveal more than I intended?**

   Backgrounds matter. Monitors, whiteboards, documents visible in photos—all can leak information.

4. **When in doubt, don't post.**

   The cost of silence is zero. The cost of exposure could be millions (and your career).

Remember: even tagging a location, a client, or a project milestone can reveal competitive intelligence.

Judy learned this the hard way. You don't have to.

What Judy's whiteboard revealed:

- Three client names (visible in upper left corner)

- Q4 launch timeline (clearly marked)

- Pricing strategy discussions (sticky notes on right side)

- Feature prioritization (diagram in center)

"I was so focused on the diagram—the clever solution we'd designed—that I didn't see everything else in the photo," Judy said. "The competitor saw it immediately."

Tone, Intent, and Professional Credibility

LinkedIn isn't Twitter. It's not Instagram. The tone you use here shapes how people perceive your professional judgment.

Research confirms this with striking specificity:

A Harvard Business Review (2024b) study showed that posts perceived as emotionally charged or self-congratulatory reduced perceived leadership credibility by 23%—even when the content itself was positive.

Conversely, posts that expressed gratitude, shared lessons, or credited teams increased perceived trustworthiness by 41%.

Translation: how you say something matters as much as what you say.

What Undermines Credibility:

✖ The Humble-Brag:
"I'm humbled to announce I've been named to the Top 40 Under 40 list . . ."
You're not humbled. You're proud. Just own it with grace.

✖ The Vague-Post:
"Exciting things happening . . . can't share yet but stay tuned 👀"
Either share or don't. Teasing feels performative.

✖ The Shock-Value Take:
"Unpopular opinion: [deliberately controversial statement designed to provoke]"
61% of professionals say sensationalism reduces trust—LinkedIn B2B Trust Survey, 2024

✖ The Personal Attack:
"People who think [X] are idiots."
Disagree with ideas, not people. Professional debate builds credibility; personal attacks destroy it.

What Builds Credibility:

☑ **Gratitude with Specificity:**

"I'm grateful to have been selected for [honor]. This recognition belongs equally to [mentor/team] who took a chance on me when I was [specific situation]. Here's what they taught me . . ."

☑ **Vulnerability with Insight:**

"I made a significant mistake on a client project last quarter. Here's what went wrong, what I learned, and how it changed my approach . . ."

☑ **Contribution Over Announcement:**

"Three lessons from leading a cross-functional team for the first time: [insights]. What would you add?"

☑ **Credit with Generosity:**

"Our team just achieved [result]. Credit goes to [specific people] who [specific contributions]. Proud to work alongside people who [values]."

See the pattern? It's not what you achieved—it's how you frame it.

Professionalism isn't censorship. It's discernment.

It's the difference between sounding confident and sounding arrogant.

Between sharing success and showing off.

Between building trust and eroding it.

Social Media Advocacy: Asset or Liability?

When employees post responsibly about their work, they become their organization's most credible ambassadors.

When they post recklessly, they become reputational liabilities.

The difference isn't whether you post about your company—it's how.

Research by Sprout Social (2024) found that 64% of consumers trust a company more when its employees share genuine content about their work.

But here's the risk: 22% of employees admit to posting company content without understanding compliance or disclosure rules (PwC Digital Trust Survey, 2024).

How to Advocate Effectively (Without Creating Risk):

1. **Disclose affiliations transparently**

   "I'm proud to work on this initiative at [Company]" or "Full disclosure: I work for [Company], but this perspective is my own."

2. **Never make unapproved claims about company performance**

   ✖ Don't say: "We're the fastest-growing company in our sector."

   ☑ Do say: "Proud to be part of a team that's growing and learning fast."

3. **Celebrate values, not just victories**

   Share stories that reflect collaboration, learning, culture—not marketing slogans or sales pitches.

4. **When in doubt, check with your communications or compliance team**

   Most companies have social media guidelines. If you're not sure, ask. Five minutes of clarification prevents years of regret.

5. **Remember: you're a team member, not a spokesperson**

   Unless you're authorized to speak on behalf of the company, make it clear you're sharing personal perspectives: "These views are my own."

The test: Would your post make your company's PR team proud or panic?

If proud: post it.

If panic: don't.

Responsible advocacy turns you into an asset. Reckless advocacy turns you into a liability.

Four Common Boundary Scenarios (Solved)

Scenario 1: Posting About Internal Projects

✖ **Don't:**

"Just wrapped up our new AI feature that predicts customer churn with 94% accuracy. Can't wait for the official launch!"

Problem: Reveals unreleased feature, specific metric, competitive intelligence

☑ **Do:**

"Spent the last quarter working on machine learning applications for customer retention. The problem-solving process taught me three things about data quality . . ."
Solution: Shares learning without revealing specifics

Scenario 2: Engaging with Senior Leaders

✘ **Don't:**

"Amazing insights from our CEO today! So inspiring! 🙌 @CEO"
Problem: Feels performative, adds no value, looks like you're trying to get noticed

☑ **Do:**

"Appreciated [CEO's] point about balancing innovation with execution. In my experience with [general project type], I've found that [specific insight]. What's worked for others?"
Solution: Adds perspective, demonstrates thinking, invites dialogue

Scenario 3: Sharing Personal Views on Sensitive Issues

✘ **Don't:**

"My company believes [political stance]. Proud to work somewhere that stands for [controversial position]."
Problem: Attributes your view to your employer without authorization

☑ **Do:**

"My experience working in [field] has taught me that [perspective based on professional experience]. This is my personal view, informed by [specific work context]."
Solution: Speaks from experience, clarifies it's personal, grounds it in work without claiming company endorsement

Scenario 4: Using AI for Content Creation

✘ **Don't:**

Post AI-generated content without disclosure, or use AI to leave automated comments on others' posts.

Problem: LinkedIn's terms prohibit automation for engagement; lack of disclosure undermines trust

☑ **Do:**

"I used AI to help structure this framework, but the insights come from [specific experience]. Here's what I learned . . ."

Solution: Transparent about AI use, ensures factual accuracy, maintains authenticity

The Five-Question Ethics Checklist

Before you hit "Post," ask yourself:

1. ☐ **Is this true, respectful, and useful?**
   If it fails any one of these tests, don't post it.

2. ☐ **Does it align with both my personal values and my company's values?**
   If there's misalignment, reconsider your framing or don't post.

3. ☐ **Could this be interpreted as disclosing confidential or proprietary information?**
   When in doubt, assume yes. Don't post it.

4. ☐ **Would I be comfortable if this post were shown in a board meeting—or printed on the front page of an industry publication?**
   If the answer is no, don't post it.

5. ☐ **Am I using my platform to build trust, or am I using it to get attention?**
   If it's the latter, pause. Reflection is the foundation of professional integrity.
   If you hesitate on any question, that hesitation is data. Listen to it.

   Judy's checklist now:

   "Before I post anything, I literally run through these five questions. If I hesitate on even one, I don't post. The three seconds it takes to think could save me three years of regret."

The Future: Ethics as Competitive Advantage

As AI-generated content, deepfakes, and algorithmic amplification become more sophisticated, authenticity is becoming a scarce asset.

According to Deloitte's 2025 Digital Ethics Forecast, organizations that train employees in responsible digital engagement experience 30% higher trust ratings and 20% lower turnover.

For employees, this means: your ethical fluency is becoming a differentiator.

The professionals who understand how to navigate boundaries with confidence—who can be authentic without being reckless, influential without being self-promotional, visible without being vulnerable to risk—those are the professionals who will build lasting careers.

Ethics aren't constraints. They're the foundation of credibility.

Boundaries don't limit expression. They define it.

And in a world where everyone has a microphone, the professionals who use it wisely will be the ones people actually want to hear from.

19 Mindset, Resilience, and Longevity: Sustaining Your LinkedIn Presence

The Quiet Hours

There's a pianist named Angela Hewitt who has performed Bach's complete keyboard works more than any living musician. She's played the Goldberg Variations in concert halls from Tokyo to London, recorded over fifty albums, and been celebrated as one of the finest Bach interpreters of her generation.

If you ask her about the secret to her mastery, she doesn't talk about talent or inspiration.

She talks about Tuesday mornings.

Every Tuesday morning for thirty years, Hewitt has sat at her piano and practiced scales. Not the Goldberg Variations. Not the Italian Concerto. Not the pieces that fill concert halls.

Scales.

The most basic, repetitive exercises a musician can do—the same patterns a beginner learns in their first lesson.

When interviewers express surprise at this routine, she looks puzzled, as if they've asked why she breathes.

"How else," she asks, "would I maintain my technique?"

This is the paradox of mastery: the world celebrates the performance, but the performance depends entirely on the practice.

Psychologists call it the 10,000-hour principle—the idea that excellence isn't a burst of genius but the accumulation of deliberate effort, one quiet hour at a time.

The same principle applies to building a LinkedIn presence.

Success isn't born from a single viral post or a month of intense activity. It's built in the quiet habit of showing up—refining, reflecting, repeating—even when no one seems to be watching.

Behind every sustainable LinkedIn presence lies an emotional rhythm: the excitement of early momentum, the pressure of consistency, the inevitable moments of fatigue and doubt.

For employees who want their presence to last rather than flicker and fade, they need three things:

> The right mindset.
>
> Resilience in the face of challenge.
>
> Strategies that support longevity.

These aren't glamorous topics. But neither are Tuesday morning scales.

And yet, these are what separate the professionals who build lasting influence from those who burn bright for three months and disappear.

The Burnout Trap (And Why Good Intentions Aren't Enough)

In 2023, researchers studying workplace behavior noticed something alarming.

They were analyzing survey responses from communications professionals—the very people whose job is to maintain corporate social media presence—and discovered that 64% reported experiencing burnout or significant exhaustion linked to constant digital engagement.

The number itself wasn't surprising. What was surprising was the pattern beneath it.

When researchers dug deeper, they discovered that burnout wasn't correlated with how much time people spent on social media during work hours.

It was correlated with how much they used social media for work during non-work hours.

The evenings. The weekends. The moments that should have been recovery time—spent instead responding to comments, checking notifications, wondering if they should post something because it had been three days.

Here's where it gets interesting:

The researchers also measured something called resilience—the capacity to bounce back from setbacks, maintain perspective under pressure, and separate identity from outcomes.

When they analyzed the data, they found that resilience didn't just help people cope with the stress of constant engagement. It fundamentally changed the relationship between social media use and burnout.

For people with low resilience, excessive social media use during non-work hours predicted turnover intention with a correlation of 0.14 (statistically significant at $p < 0.01$).

But for people with high resilience, that relationship weakened dramatically.

Resilience, in other words, wasn't just a nice-to-have trait. It was a protective factor.

This is what we might call the burnout trap:

Visibility on social media is fleeting—a post appears, generates engagement for a few hours, then vanishes into the algorithmic void. But credibility is cumulative. It compounds over time.

The challenge is figuring out how to build credibility without falling into the trap of constant presence without boundaries.

The solution has less to do with tactics than with mindset.

The First Mindset Shift: From Obligation to Purpose

Consider two professionals who both commit to posting on LinkedIn once a week:

Professional A posts because they've heard LinkedIn is good for their career. They don't have a clear sense of why they're posting or what they hope to achieve. They just know they "should" be doing it.

Every Saturday morning feels like an assignment. They stare at a blank screen, wondering what to write, feeling pressure to say something impressive. Posting feels like a chore.

Professional B posts because they want to contribute to a specific conversation in their field. They have questions they're genuinely curious about, insights developed through their work, and a desire to connect with people who share their interests.

For this person, posting isn't a task to check off. It's an extension of their professional identity.

Which person do you think is still posting six months later?

The answer, based on research into motivation and sustained behavior, is almost certainly Professional B.

Daniel Kahneman, the Nobel Prize-winning psychologist, observed that we are pattern-seeking animals. We look for narratives that explain our behavior, and those narratives—whether accurate or not—shape our future choices.

When your "why" is clear, the "how often" becomes easier.

When you're driven by external pressure—by the sense that you *should* be doing something—consistency feels like a burden.

When you're driven by internal purpose—by genuine curiosity, contribution, or connection—consistency feels like continuation.

This is the first mindset shift required for longevity: moving from obligation to contribution.

Ask yourself: Why am I posting?

Not "Why should I post?" but "Why do I *want* to post?"

Is it to:

- Share what you're learning to help others avoid your mistakes?

- Think through complex problems by articulating them publicly?

- Connect with people whose work inspires you?

- Document your professional journey for future reflection?

- Build credibility in a specific domain you care about?

The specifics matter less than the clarity.

When you know why you're showing up, you can make better decisions about when to push forward and when to pull back. You can weather the weeks when engagement is low because you're not posting for engagement—you're posting for purpose.

Sarah Chen, the product manager we met in earlier chapters, posts every Tuesday at 7:15 AM. When asked why she maintains this rhythm even when life gets busy, she doesn't talk about growth strategies or algorithms.

"Tuesday mornings," she says, "are when I process the previous week and prepare for the next one. Posting is how I think. If I stopped, I'd lose something valuable—not followers, but clarity."

That's purpose. And purpose is what sustains you when metrics don't.

The Second Mindset Shift: From Perfection to Growth

In another study focused on enterprise social media use, researchers found something counterintuitive:

Employees with high communication visibility on internal platforms actually reported greater resilience and better adaptation under pressure.

At first glance, this seems to contradict the burnout findings. More visibility equals more stress, right?

Not exactly.

The key variable was how people approached their visibility.

When employees viewed their online presence as a performance—something that needed to be perfect, impressive, curated—the cognitive load was exhausting.

But when they viewed it as a conversation—something that could evolve, include mistakes, and invite feedback—the experience was energizing rather than draining.

This distinction maps onto one of the most common obstacles people face when building a LinkedIn presence: perfectionism.

The belief that every post needs to be polished. Every comment needs to be clever. Every interaction needs to be impressive.

But perfectionism is the enemy of consistency. And consistency is what builds credibility.

Consider the alternative mindset: growth over perfection.

Accept that early posts may not land perfectly. What matters is the compound effect of insights you build over time.

> Your first ten posts are practice.
>
> Your first fifty posts are education.
>
> Your first hundred posts are when you start finding your voice.

When Sarah Chen looks back at her early LinkedIn posts, she winces slightly. The tone was too formal. The insights were obvious. The structure was clunky.

But she didn't delete them. She kept them as evidence of evolution.

"If I look back and don't cringe a little," she says, "it means I haven't grown."

This is what psychologists call a growth mindset, and it's essential for sustained presence on any platform.

You're not performing. You're practicing.

The goal isn't to be impressive today. It's to be better tomorrow than you were today.

The permission slip you need:

Your 47th post can be better than your 12th post. Your voice in Year 2 can sound different from your voice in Month 3. Evolution isn't failure—it's the whole point.

Give yourself permission to be a beginner at the beginning.

The Boundary Imperative

Let's return to those burned-out communications professionals.

The researchers identified something crucial: resilience wasn't just an innate personality trait. It could be built through specific practices.

And the most effective practice was surprisingly simple: setting boundaries.

The people who maintained engagement without burning out had clear rules about when and how they used social media for work:

- They didn't check LinkedIn notifications constantly

- They didn't feel obligated to respond to every comment immediately

- They had designated times for posting and engaging

- They protected their off-hours with the same vigilance they protected meeting time

This might sound obvious, but consider how rare it is in practice.

The default behavior for most people on social media is reactive: a notification arrives, and they respond. A thought occurs, and they post. Someone comments, and they feel obligated to reply immediately.

This creates what researchers call an "always-on" mentality—a state of continuous partial attention that's exhausting to maintain and impossible to sustain.

The alternative is to be deliberate rather than reactive.

Here's what that looks like in practice:

1. **Set a posting rhythm you can sustain for a year, not just a month**
   For many employees, that means one thoughtful post every week or two, not daily bursts that lead to burnout.
   Decide *when* you'll post—Saturday mornings with coffee, Tuesday evenings after dinner, whatever works for your schedule—and block that time in your calendar like any other important commitment.

2. **Give yourself permission to schedule rest**
   Take one week per quarter where you skip posting but still engage with others' content. Use it as a refresh period.

When posting starts to feel like a burden rather than a contribution, you're at risk of burnout. Adjust before you crash.

3. **Create response boundaries**

You don't need to reply to every comment within five minutes. Set a window: "I'll respond to comments within 24 hours, but not immediately."

This trains your audience to expect thoughtful responses, not instant reactions.

4. **Track your emotional reaction**

This is the canary in the coal mine.

Are your posts adding to your professional joy or adding to your stress?

If posting used to energize you but now drains you, something needs to change. Maybe it's your posting frequency. Maybe it's your content pillars. Maybe it's your expectation of what success looks like.

But pay attention to the signal before it becomes a crisis.

The Idea Bank Strategy (Never Start from Scratch Again)

There's a writer named Austin Kleon who has published a newsletter every week for more than a decade.

When people ask how he maintains that consistency, he shows them a folder on his computer labeled **"Seeds."**

It contains thousands of notes—observations, quotes, photos, half-formed thoughts—collected over years.

When it's time to write, he doesn't start from scratch. He waters the seeds.

This is one of the most effective strategies for sustained LinkedIn presence: archive ideas continuously.

Your calendar, your meetings, your photos, your conversations—these are all story sources. The challenge isn't finding ideas. It's capturing them before they evaporate.

How to build your idea bank:

Keep a running note on your phone (or Notion, Evernote, whatever works)

When you notice something interesting in a meeting, write it down.

When a colleague asks a smart question, save it.

When you solve a problem, document the lesson.

When you read something that sparks a reaction, capture the thought.

Organize by content pillars (optional but helpful)

If your pillars are Leadership, Supply Chain Innovation, and Team Culture, tag ideas accordingly. When it's time to post about leadership, you have a dozen ready-made starting points.

Over time, you'll have a reservoir of potential posts. You'll never face a blank page on Saturday morning wondering "What should I write?"

This transforms the creative process from generation to curation.

Instead of asking "What should I post about?" you're asking "Which of these ten ideas feels most relevant right now?"

That's a fundamentally easier question to answer, and it dramatically reduces the cognitive load of consistent posting.

Sarah Chen's idea bank has 147 entries. Some are single sentences. Some are photos with brief notes. Some are frameworks sketched on napkins.

"I'll never use all of them," she says. "But knowing they're there means I never feel stuck. I'm choosing, not creating from nothing."

The Evolution Paradox

Here's something nobody tells you about building a sustained LinkedIn presence:

Sometime around month six or twelve, you'll feel like your voice has gone stale.

Your format will feel repetitive. Your topics will feel exhausted. Your engagement might even decline slightly. You'll wonder if you've said everything you have to say.

This is not a sign of failure. This is a sign of growth.

When you start posting, you're learning the basics—how to structure a post, how to engage comments, how to find your rhythm. Those early months require effort because you're building new skills.

But once you've mastered the basics, they stop feeling challenging. They start feeling mechanical. Your brain, which thrives on novelty and challenge, begins to disengage.

The solution isn't to quit. It's to evolve deliberately.

Ways to evolve your presence:

Try a new format

If you've been writing text posts, try carousels. If you've mastered carousels, try video. If you've been doing solo posts, interview someone in your network and share their insights.

Explore a new content pillar

Adjacent to your current topics, not wildly different. If you write about marketing strategy, start exploring customer psychology. If you write about leadership, start exploring team dynamics.

Document learning, not just teaching

Instead of writing about what you know, write about what you're currently figuring out. Share experiments, half-formed ideas, questions you don't have answers to.

The specific change matters less than the act of changing.

Sarah Chen experienced this around month nine. Her product management posts were still performing well numerically, but she felt like she was repeating herself.

So she made a shift: instead of writing about what she knew, she started writing about what she was learning. She documented experiments in progress, shared ideas that might be wrong, and asked questions she didn't have answers to.

Her engagement didn't spike immediately. But something more valuable happened: she started enjoying posting again.

And her audience noticed the shift. The comments became longer, more thoughtful, more conversational. She had evolved from teacher to learner, and paradoxically, that made her more valuable as a voice in her field.

Permission to evolve: Your voice at Month 18 doesn't need to sound like your voice at Month 3. Evolution is not abandoning your positioning—it's deepening it.

The Compound Effect (Why Longevity Beats Intensity)

There's a financial concept called **compound interest**: the idea that small, consistent investments grow exponentially over time.

A dollar invested today doesn't just earn interest. It earns interest on the interest. The growth curve starts slowly, then accelerates.

The same principle applies to LinkedIn presence.

Your first post reaches your immediate network—maybe fifty people.

Your tenth post reaches a slightly wider circle because the algorithm has learned what you write about.

Your fiftieth post reaches people you've never met because your content has been shared, saved, and recommended.

But here's the critical insight: the compound effect only works if you stay in the game.

If you post enthusiastically for three months, burn out, and disappear for six months, you're starting over every time.

The algorithm forgets you.

Your audience forgets you.

You never benefit from compounding.

This is why longevity matters more than intensity.

One thoughtful post per week for a year beats three posts per day for a month.

Consistency compounds. Intensity doesn't.

Think about Sarah Chen: 70,000 people now see her Tuesday morning posts. But in her first month, those posts reached 200 people. In Month 6, they reached 800. In Month 12, they reached 4,000.

The growth wasn't linear. It was exponential. But only because she stayed consistent.

If she'd burned out at Month 6, she'd never have reached Month 12's compounding effect.

The math of compounding presence:

Month 1–3: Building foundation (slow, sometimes discouraging)

Month 4–6: Early momentum (starting to see familiar names)

Month 7–12: Compound effect begins (opportunities start arriving)

Year 2+: Established presence (system works for you)

Most people quit somewhere between Months 3 and 6, right before compounding kicks in.

Don't be most people.

The Longevity Playbook (Your Practical Framework)

Let's make this actionable. Here's your framework for sustained LinkedIn presence:

1. **Set Your Cadence**

   Decide your posting rhythm—every Saturday morning, every other Tuesday evening—and block it in your calendar. Treat it like a meeting with yourself.

2. **Use Mini-Rituals**

   Create a simple routine around posting: thirty minutes with coffee, review the week, pick one insight to share. Rituals reduce decision fatigue.

3. **Maintain an Idea Bank**

   Keep 50–100 potential story prompts from your work, photos, calendar. When it's time to post, you're curating rather than creating from scratch.

4. **Review Quarterly**

   What landed? What didn't? Update your content pillars based on evidence, not intuition.

5. **Schedule Rest**

   One week per quarter, skip posting but engage with others' content. Use it as a refresh period.

6. **Celebrate Progress**

   Note when profile views rise, when leadership comments, when opportunities arrive. Create a success log to counter negativity bias.

7. **Check Your Alignment**

   If you feel fatigue, pause and ask: Am I still aligned with my "why"? Am I posting for visibility or value?

8. **Evolve Deliberately**

   Every six to nine months, try one new thing: format, topic, approach. Keep what works, discard what doesn't.

This isn't a productivity hack. It's a sustainability framework.

And sustainability is what separates people who build lasting presence from people who burn bright and fade.

Final Thoughts: The Endurance Principle

Angela Hewitt, the pianist, has been asked many times why she still practices scales after thirty years of performing at the highest level.

Her answer is instructive:

"The moment I stop practicing is the moment I stop improving. And if I stop improving, I stop enjoying it."

Longevity on LinkedIn isn't glamorous. It's not about viral moments or explosive growth or being featured in someone's "Top 10 LinkedIn Influencers" list.

It's quiet. It's consistent. It's showing up when you feel busy, when results aren't instant, when engagement is low—but staying present anyway because you believe in the value you bring.

Your voice today may sound different from your voice a year from now, and that's not just okay—that's the whole point. Evolution is part of presence.

The most enduring posts aren't the ones that stood out for a moment. They're the ones that stood the test of time.

When you combine purpose, resilience, and sustainability, you'll build not just a presence—you'll build a professional legacy.

Because in the end, the people who succeed on LinkedIn aren't the ones who went viral once.

They're the ones who showed up every Tuesday morning, practiced their scales, and never stopped learning.

That's Angela Hewitt.

That's Sarah Chen.

That can be you.

EPILOGUE FROM PRESENCE TO LEGACY

That Tuesday afternoon in 2018 seems like a lifetime ago now.

I was sitting at my kitchen table, staring at a blank text box on LinkedIn, terrified to hit publish. I didn't know if anyone would read it. I didn't know if I had anything valuable to say. I didn't know if showing up publicly, as myself, would help or hurt my career.

I just knew I was tired of being invisible.

The post I finally published that evening wasn't brilliant. It wasn't viral. Eleven people liked it—eight I knew personally, three probably by accident. But those eleven people represented something I couldn't achieve through email, through meetings, through the traditional channels of corporate communication.

They represented a start.

Six years later, I have over 80,000 followers. My posts reach millions of people annually. I've been recognized as a LinkedIn Top Voice, ranked among the top voices globally in my field.

But here's what matters more than any of those numbers:

I've had conversations with professionals across six continents about markets, leadership, and purpose. I've received messages from young analysts saying a post helped them think through a career decision. I've been invited to speak, to collaborate, to contribute in ways that wouldn't have been possible if I'd stayed silent.

And inside my own organization, I'm no longer just a name on an email thread. I'm a voice. My ideas travel further. My influence extends deeper. Not because I became more competent at my job, but because I made my competence visible.

That's what LinkedIn gave me. Not fame. Not followers.

It gave me a bridge between who I am and who I want to be. Between the insights I develop privately and the impact I can create publicly. Between the limitations of organizational hierarchy and the possibilities of professional community.

I need to be honest about something: the numbers feel good.

When a post gets 10,000 views, when hundreds of people engage with an idea, when someone messages to say your framework helped them—it's validating. It's encouraging. It's proof that showing up matters.

But I've also learned that the numbers are the least important part of this journey.

The most important part is the person you become in the process of building a presence. The discipline of thinking clearly enough to communicate publicly. The humility of admitting when you're wrong or still learning. The generosity of sharing insights without expecting anything in return. The resilience of posting when engagement is low, when critics emerge, when it feels like nobody's paying attention.

LinkedIn didn't just build my network. It built up to who I am becoming.

Your Tuesday Afternoon Is Waiting

Somewhere right now, someone is sitting where I sat six years ago.

They're staring at a blank text box. They're wondering if they have anything valuable to say. They're afraid of judgment, of silence, of exposure.

They're stuck in that moment between intention and action, between who they are and who they could become.

If that's you, I want you to know something:

You don't need permission. You don't need a perfect first post. You don't need thousands of followers before you start.

You just need to begin.

APPENDIX QUICK-START RESOURCES

Thirty-Day LinkedIn Launch Plan

Week 1: Foundation

- Day 1–2: Audit your profile (photo, headline, About section)

- Day 3–4: Identify your content pillars (three to five themes)

- Day 5–7: Define your value proposition and audience

Week 2: Setup and Observation

- Day 8–9: Update profile with new headline and About section

- Day 10–11: Follow twenty to thirty voices in your field

- Day 12–14: Observe and comment on others' posts (practice engagement)

Week 3: First Posts

- Day 15: Publish your first post (keep it simple)

- Day 17: Publish second post (different pillar)

- Day 19: Publish third post (rotate format)

- Day 16, 18, 20, 21: Engage with comments and others' content

Week 4: Rhythm and Reflection

- Day 22: Publish fourth post

- Day 24: Publish fifth post

- Day 26–28: Engage actively, respond to comments

- Day 29–30: Review analytics, note what worked, plan next month

Content Pillar Worksheet

Your Expertise: What are you genuinely good at? What problems do people come to you to solve?

Your Interests: What topics energize you? What do you read about for fun?

Your Audience's Needs: What challenges do your peers, clients, or team face?

Your Content Pillars (three to five themes):

Pillar 1: _________________ Why it matters to you: Example post ideas:

Pillar 2: _________________ Why it matters to you: Example post ideas:

Pillar 3: _________________ Why it matters to you: Example post ideas:

Pillar 4: _________________ Why it matters to you: Example post ideas:

Pillar 5: _________________ Why it matters to you: Example post ideas:

Monthly Planning Template

Month: _________________

Content Focus: Which pillar(s) will you emphasize this month?

Post Schedule:

- Week 1: [Date] - [Topic/Pillar]

- Week 2: [Date] - [Topic/Pillar]

- Week 3: [Date] - [Topic/Pillar]

- Week 4: [Date] - [Topic/Pillar]

Engagement Goals:

- Comment on ____ posts per week

- Respond to all comments within ____ hours

- Connect with ____ new people this month

Experiments to Try:

- New format (carousel, video, poll)?

- New posting time?

- New topic adjacent to your pillars?

Success Metrics to Track:

- Profile views

- Post impressions

- Engagement rate

- Meaningful conversations started

Quarterly Audit Framework

Quarter: __________________

Metrics Review:

- Average post impressions: _____________

- Average engagement rate: ____________

- Profile views (total): ____________

- Follower growth: ____________

- Meaningful opportunities: ____________

What Worked:

- Top three posts and why they resonated:
- Best format:
- Best timing:
- Most engaged pillar:

What Didn't Work:

- Posts that underperformed and why:
- Topics to avoid or reframe:
- Formats that didn't land:

Insights and Adjustments:

- What did you learn about your audience?
- What will you do differently next quarter?
- Any pivots to your content pillars?

Personal Reflection:

- How does posting feel? (Energizing/draining?)
- Are you still aligned with your why?
- What boundaries need adjusting?

GLOSSARY OF LINKEDIN TERMS

A

Algorithm   The system that determines which posts appear in users' feeds and in what order

C

Carousel   Multi-slide post format (PDF/images) that users swipe through

Connection   Someone in your first-degree network

Creator Mode   Profile setting that unlocks additional features (newsletters, live video, and featured topics)

D

Dwell Time   How long someone spends reading your post (key algorithm signal)

E

Engagement Rate   Ratio of interactions (likes, comments, and shares) to impressions

F

Featured Section   Area on profile to showcase key posts, articles, or media

Follower   Someone who sees your public posts without being connected

I

Impressions   Number of times your post was displayed

S

Save   When someone bookmarks your post (strong value signal to algorithm)

Social Proof   Evidence that others trust/value you (recommendations, endorsements, and testimonials)

T

Thought Leadership   Content that demonstrates expertise and adds value to professional conversations

V

Value Proposition   Clear statement of who you help, what outcome you deliver, and how

BIBLIOGRAPHY

Academic Research and Journal Articles

Bower, Gordon H. (1977). "Mood-Congruent Memory." *Journal of Experimental Psychology: General*, 106(3), 236–255.

Cialdini, Robert B. (2006). *Influence: The Psychology of Persuasion* (Revised Edition). New York: Harper Business.

Cowan, Nelson (2010). "The Magical Mystery Four: How Is Working Memory Capacity Limited, and Why?" *Current Directions in Psychological Science*, 19(1), 51–57.

Duckworth, Angela L., Peterson, Christopher, Matthews, Michael D., & Kelly, Dennis R. (2007). "Grit: Perseverance and Passion for Long-Term Goals." *Journal of Personality and Social Psychology*, 92(6), 1087–1101.

Ericsson, K. Anders, Krampe, Ralf T., & Tesch-Römer, Clemens (2008). "The Role of Deliberate Practice in the Acquisition of Expert Performance." *Psychological Review*, 100(3), 363–406.

Festinger, Leon (1954). "A Theory of Social Comparison Processes." *Human Relations*, 7(2), 117–140.

Granovetter, Mark S. (1973). "The Strength of Weak Ties." *American Journal of Sociology*, 78(6), 1360–1380.

Gruber, Matthias J., Gelman, Bernard D., & Ranganath, Charan (2014). "States of Curiosity Modulate Hippocampus-Dependent Learning via the Dopaminergic Circuit." *Neuron*, 84(2), 486–496.

Hasson, Uri, Ghazanfar, Asif A., Galantucci, Bruno, Garrod, Simon, & Keysers, Christian (2010). "Brain-to-Brain Coupling: A Mechanism for Creating and Sharing a Social World." *Trends in Cognitive Sciences*, 16(2), 114–121.

Kahneman, Daniel (2011). *Thinking, Fast and Slow.* New York: Farrar, Straus and Giroux.

Miller, George A. (1956). "The Magical Number Seven, Plus or Minus Two: Some Limits on Our Capacity for Processing Information." *Psychological Review,* 63(2), 81–97.

Norton, Michael I., Mochon, Daniel, & Ariely, Dan (2012). "The IKEA Effect: When Labor Leads to Love." *Journal of Consumer Psychology,* 22(3), 453–460.

Pascual-Leone, Alvaro, Nguyet, Dang, Cohen, Leonardo G., Brasil-Neto, Joaquim P., Cammarota, Angel, & Hallett, Mark (1995). "Modulation of Muscle Responses Evoked by Transcranial Magnetic Stimulation During the Acquisition of New Fine Motor Skills." *Journal of Neurophysiology,* 74(3), 1037–1045.

Prochaska, James O., & DiClemente, Carlo C. (2001). "The Transtheoretical Approach." In *Handbook of Psychotherapy Integration* (2nd ed., pp. 147–171). New York: Oxford University Press.

Putnam, Robert D. (2000). *Bowling Alone: The Collapse and Revival of American Community.* New York: Simon & Schuster.

Zajonc, Robert B. (1968). "Attitudinal Effects of Mere Exposure." *Journal of Personality and Social Psychology,* 9(2, Pt.2), 1–27.

Books and Published Works

Clear, James (2018). *Atomic Habits: An Easy & Proven Way to Build Good Habits & Break Bad Ones.* New York: Avery.

Csikszentmihalyi, Mihaly (1990). *Flow: The Psychology of Optimal Experience.* New York: Harper & Row.

Gladwell, Malcolm (2000). *The Tipping Point: How Little Things Can Make a Big Difference.* Boston: Little, Brown and Company.

Heath, Chip, & Heath, Dan (2007). *Made to Stick: Why Some Ideas Survive and Others Die.* New York: Random House.

Kleon, Austin (2012). *Steal Like an Artist: 10 Things Nobody Told You About Being Creative.* New York: Workman Publishing.

Levitt, Theodore (1960). "Marketing Myopia." *Harvard Business Review,* 38(4), 45–56.

LinkedIn Data and Platform Research

LinkedIn (2019). "Trust in Professional Networks Study." LinkedIn Member Research.

LinkedIn (2024a). "Comment Engagement Study: Comments Drive 30-75× More Views Than Likes." LinkedIn Algorithm Research.

LinkedIn (2024b). "Creator Analytics Report 2024." LinkedIn Internal Data.

LinkedIn (2024c). "Engagement Rate Benchmarks: Median 4.73%, Smaller Accounts Average 6%." LinkedIn Creator Analytics.

LinkedIn (2024d). "Profile Completeness Impact Study: 40× More Opportunities with Complete Profiles." LinkedIn Data Science Team.

LinkedIn (2024e). "Top Voice Program Methodology." LinkedIn Creator Program.

LinkedIn Algorithm Update (2024). "Platform Shift: Saves, Shares, and Dwell Time Weighted More Heavily Than Likes; Posts with High Dwell Time Receive 3× More Organic Reach."

LinkedIn B2B Marketing Study (2024). "Trust as Factor in B2B Decision-Making: 93.7% of Decision-Makers Prioritize Trust."

LinkedIn B2B Trust Survey (2024). "61% Say Sensationalism Reduces Trust in Professional Context."

LinkedIn Engagement Report (2024). "Story-Based Posts Generate 58% More Comments Than Generic Announcements."

LinkedIn Groups Data (2024). "100 Million+ Users Engage in LinkedIn Groups Monthly."

LinkedIn Marketing Solutions (2024). "Employee Advocacy Reach Study: 561% Greater Reach for Employee-Shared Content."

LinkedIn Newsletter Statistics (2024). "184,000+ Active Newsletters; 47% Engagement Increase for Newsletter Subscribers vs. Regular Followers."

LinkedIn Thought Leadership Index (2024). "Emotional Tension in Content Increases Attention Span by 2.5×; Posts with Emotional Narrative Hold Attention 40-60% Longer."

LinkedIn/Ipsos (2024). "Thought Leadership and Influence Study: 93% Say Trust Matters More Than Reach."

Industry Reports and Workforce Surveys

CareerBuilder (2023). "Social Media Recruitment Survey: 90% of Employers Review Social Media Profiles Before Hiring or Promotion Decisions."

CIPD (Chartered Institute of Personnel and Development) (2023). "Social Media Discipline Survey: 25% of HR Professionals Have Disciplined Employees for Social Media Misconduct."

Deloitte (2025). "Digital Ethics Forecast: Organizations with Digital Ethics Training Experience 30% Higher Trust Ratings and 20% Lower Turnover."

Deloitte Ethics & Compliance Report (2024). "42% of Employers Report at Least One Reputational or Compliance Incident in Past Year Linked to Employee Online Behavior."

Deloitte Risk Advisory (2023). "Data Leak Study: 68% of Data-Leak Incidents Involving Employees Began with Non-Malicious Intent."

Edelman Trust Barometer (2012, 2019, 2024). "Trust in Institutions and Spokespersons: Regular Employees Trusted 52% vs. CEOs 38%."

Edelman Trust Barometer (2024a). "Competence and Ethics Drive 88% of Perceived Trust in Professional Interactions."

Edelman Trust Barometer (2024b). "Professionals Demonstrating Humility and Authenticity Online: 47% More Credible Than Accomplishment-Only Profiles."

Hootsuite Social Trends Report (2025). "32% of Employees Report Being Unsure Where Employer Brand Ends and Personal Brand Begins."

IBM Cost of Insider Threats Report (2024). "Unintentional Data Disclosure Costs Companies Average $4.9 Million per Incident, Up 11% from Previous Year."

Jobvite (2023). "Recruiter Screening Study: Most Recruiters Decide Within 6 Seconds Whether a LinkedIn Profile Is Worth Reading; 77% Use LinkedIn as Primary Tool."

Nielsen Consumer Trust Index (2012). "92% of People Trust Recommendations from Individuals (Even Strangers) Over Branded Messages."

Psychology Today (2023). "Facial Expression Research: Faces with Genuine Smiles Rated as More Approachable and Trustworthy."

PwC Digital Trust Survey (2024). "22% of Employees Admit to Posting Company Content Without Understanding Compliance or Disclosure Rules."

PwC Global Workforce Survey (2024). "70% of Professionals Say a Colleague's Online Behavior Affects Their Perception of That Person at Work."

Social Insider (2024). "Multi-Slide Carousels Increase Viewing Duration by 3× Compared to Single-Image Posts."

SocialPilot (2025). "LinkedIn Format Engagement Study: Multi-Image Carousels Average 6.60% Engagement Rate—Highest of All LinkedIn Formats; Documents 6.10%; Standard Posts 3-4%."

Sprout Social (2024). "Consumer Trust Study: 64% of Consumers Trust a Company More When Employees Share Genuine Content About Their Work."

Harvard Business Review and Business Research

Harvard Business Review (2024a). "Emotional Posts Study: 70% More Memorable Than Neutral Content."

Harvard Business Review (2024b). "Leadership Credibility Study: Emotionally Charged or Self-Congratulatory Posts Reduce Perceived Leadership Credibility by 23%; Posts Expressing Gratitude Increase Trustworthiness by 41%."

Harvard Business Review (2024c). "Micro-Interactions and Career Mobility: Professionals Engaging in Short, Authentic Online Exchanges Experience Stronger Career Mobility and More Mentorship Opportunities."

Harvard Business Review Analytic Services (2024). "Online Presence Impact: Employees with Active, Credible Online Presence Perceived as 21% More Innovative and 27% More Likely to Be Seen as Future Leaders by Peers and Supervisors."

Journal of Business and Psychology (2019). "Personal Branding Behavior and Perceived Employability: Correlation Coefficient of 0.48 Between Personal Branding and Employability."

Network Science and Career Development

Behavioral Economics Research (n.d.). "Signaling Theory in Career Development: Employees Sharing Evidence of Expertise Online More Likely to Be Perceived as Competent and Promotable, Especially When Supported by Consistent Engagement and Peer Endorsement."

Network Science Research (n.d.). "Network Connectivity Impact: 10-Percentile Improvement in Network Connectivity Corresponds to 0.27-Percentile Increase in Monthly Recruiter InMails."

Media and News References

Business Standard (n.d.). Business publication referenced in Priya Sharma case study.

Economic Times (n.d.). Business publication referenced in Priya Sharma case study.

People Matters (n.d.). HR and workplace publication referenced in talent management contexts.

TechCrunch (n.d.). Technology industry news and startup coverage.

The Economist (October 2025). "LinkedIn and the Art of Self-Promotion." Analysis of self-promotion culture on professional platforms.

Technology and Cognitive Science Studies

Microsoft & University of Toronto (2015). "Attention Spans Research: Average Human Attention Span Has Decreased to 8.25 Seconds, Down from 12 Seconds in 2000."

Nielsen Norman Group (2019). "Eye-Tracking Studies: Users Read Only 20% of Text on Average Webpage; 57% of Time Spent on First Screenful of Content."

ScienceDirect (2023). "Social Proof Study: Visible Engagement Cues Increased Perceived Credibility by 32% Even When Content Was Identical."

Burnout, Resilience, and Workplace Behavior

Enterprise Social Media Study (n.d.). "Visibility and Resilience: Employees with High Communication Visibility Report Greater Resilience When Viewing Online Presence as Conversation Rather Than Performance."

Resilience Research (n.d.). "Resilience as Protective Factor: For Individuals with High Resilience, Correlation Between Excessive Non-Work Social Media Use and Turnover Intention Weakens Significantly ($p < 0.01$)."

Workplace Behavior Research (2023). "Digital Burnout Study: 64% of Communications Professionals Report Burnout or Significant Exhaustion Linked to Constant Digital Engagement."

Methodology and Research Approach

This book synthesizes:

✓ **6 years of practitioner experience** (James Cheo, 2018–2024, Singapore)
✓ **Personal case study**: 0 to 80,000+ followers as Chief Investment Officer
✓ **12+ diverse professional case studies** across nine countries, seven industries
✓ **50+ peer-reviewed academic sources** in psychology, behavioral economics, network science, organizational behavior ✓ **LinkedIn's proprietary platform research** (algorithm studies, engagement patterns, trust research) ✓ **Major consulting firm reports** (Deloitte, PwC, Edelman, IBM) ✓ **Industry surveys** (CareerBuilder, CIPD, Jobvite, Nielsen)

Character Development Approach:

All character stories are composite case studies based on:

- Real patterns observed across 500+ LinkedIn professionals

- Anonymized and adapted for instructional purposes

- Verified against actual platform data and engagement metrics

- Names changed to protect privacy while maintaining demographic diversity

ABOUT THE AUTHOR

There's a moment James Cheo remembers clearly. It was a Tuesday afternoon in 2018, and he was staring at his inbox, waiting for replies that would never come.

He'd spent three hours crafting an email about sustainability trends in emerging markets—something he thought was important, something that could reshape how his colleagues thought about investment strategy. He hit send to forty people across different regions.

Silence.

Not even an acknowledgment. The email simply vanished into the corporate void, buried under meeting invitations and budget updates.

This wasn't unusual. This was normal.

James is one employee among hundreds of thousands, scattered across time zones and continents. He has insights worth sharing, twenty-five years of investment experience to draw from, credentials that filled a line (CFA, CAIA, FRM). But expertise without visibility is just noise in a crowded room.

So he tried something different. He tried LinkedIn.

That first post received eleven likes. Eight were from people he knew personally. Three were probably accidental.

Six years later, James has built a following of over 80,000 professionals. His posts reach millions annually. He's been recognized as a LinkedIn Top Voice, ranked among the top voices globally in financial markets.

But here's what matters: he's still an employee. Not an entrepreneur. Not selling courses or building a consultancy. Just a Chief Investment Officer who wanted a voice that reached beyond his immediate circle.

From Economist to Investment Leader

James's career spans continents and crises. He started as a public-sector economist before transitioning into wealth management and investment strategy at global banks and wealth firms. Along the way, he's led award-winning investment research teams, translated market complexity into clarity for clients, and navigated everything from the 2008 financial crisis to the pandemic's market disruptions.

His professional rigor is undeniable—the kind that comes from twenty-five years of making decisions when billions are on the line. But what sets James apart isn't just his credentials. It's his refusal to hide behind them.

The Unlikely Storyteller

On LinkedIn, James doesn't write like a Chief Investment Officer. He writes like a human being who happens to work in finance.

He posts about market cycles, yes. But also about the mentor who took a chance on him when he was twenty-three and overconfident. About the day he realized listening matters more than speaking. About sustainability—not just as an investment trend, but as a personal conviction shaped by his upbringing.

This blend of professional insight and personal storytelling is what transformed his LinkedIn presence from a digital résumé into something more powerful: a platform that connects investment thinking with human stories, makes complex ideas accessible, and builds community rather than just broadcasting content.

His followers aren't just reading market analysis. They're learning how to think, how to communicate, and how to build influence without losing authenticity.

Why He Wrote This Book

James wrote *The LinkedIn Playbook for Employees* because he kept getting asked the same question: "How did you do it?"

The honest answer? He didn't do anything magical. He just did something consistently.

But there were principles behind the practice. Patterns he noticed. Mistakes he made. Lessons learned the hard way that others don't have to learn the same way.

This book isn't theory from a marketing guru or a social media consultant. It's frontline experience from someone who built a voice while working full-time, who navigated corporate boundaries while maintaining authenticity, who proved that employees don't need to become entrepreneurs to become influential.

Every chapter draws from James's dual journey—twenty-five years leading investment strategy and six years building one of the most recognized employee voices on LinkedIn. The water bottle experiment that explains branding. The neuroscience of curiosity that reveals why some posts get saved and others get scrolled past. The quiet Saturday mornings that became his content creation ritual.

What Makes This Book Different

James challenges professionals to step beyond their job titles and articulate their unique value. To stop waiting for permission and start sharing what they know. To build personal brands grounded not in self-promotion, but in service.

Whether you're an employee seeking visibility, a leader looking to amplify your influence, or a professional tired of feeling invisible in a large organization, James delivers what he's always delivered: clarity, confidence, and a pathway from presence to opportunity.

Not through hacks or algorithms. Through consistency, authenticity, and the compound effect of small actions repeated over time.

The Work Continues

Today, James lives in Singapore, where he splits his time between leading investment strategy, mentoring emerging professionals, and writing about the intersection of markets, purpose, and personal branding.

He still posts on LinkedIn every week. He still responds to comments from strangers who found value in something he shared. He still believes that the best professional advice isn't about climbing ladders—it's about building bridges.

And he still remembers that Tuesday afternoon in 2018, staring at a silent inbox, wondering if anyone would ever hear what he had to say.

The answer, it turns out, was yes. But only when he stopped sending emails and started showing up where people could actually find him.

INDEX